The Man Who Returned From The Dead

JOHN MYERS MYERS

PENGUIN BOOKS

PENGUIN BOOKS

UK | USA | Canada | Ireland | Australia
India | New Zealand | South Africa

Penguin Books is part of the Penguin Random House group of companies
whose addresses can be found at global.penguinrandomhouse.com.

Previously published as *The Saga of Hugh Glass: Pirate, Pawnee, and Mountain Man*
by Bison Books, part of the University of Nebraska Press 1976
First published in Penguin Books 2016
001

Printed in Great Britain by Clays Ltd, St Ives plc

A CIP catalogue record for this book is available from the British Library

ISBN: 978-0-718-18496-4

The Man Who Returned
From The Dead

To
Dr. Thad Morrison, Sr. —
with whom I've enjoyed
many another glass

Contents

.\\./\./\./\./\./\.

The Man Who Returned
From The Dead

Told Without Footnotes

.∧.∧.∧.∧.∧.∧.

THE LEGEND, ITS CHALLENGERS AND FOUNDATIONS

*One man who allso tore nearly all to peases by a
White Bear and was left by the way without any gun
who afterwards recover'd.*
— LETTER BY DANIEL T. POTTS

DEEP IN THE MEDICINE BAG of every nation
is the tale of a warrior pitted against a beast of
dread proportions. In the lore of America, this alpha of
epics takes the form of a struggle between a mountain
man called Hugh Glass and an outsize grizzly. The different turn taken by the story of Hugh, though, is that
the duel itself is of less moment than his feat of surviving, after being abandoned in the wilderness by men
who were sure his watch couldn't be wound again.

In common with Sigurd, Perseus and like monster
fighters, Hugh had other signal adventures, if chiefly
pegged by tradition on the score of but one. The purpose of this volume is to present as a whole the never-
before-assembled reports about a character who is by

way of being the New World's Sinbad. Whether or not any of these can also be styled "facts" will be the book's secondary concern.

That is necessary for a curious but far from unparalleled reason. The late Hugh Glass has enemies of whom he knew nothing at the time of his death, one hundred and thirty years ago. Then he only had gigantic bruins and wild Indians to deal with; but today there are literary sharpshooters ready to draw bead on any man who wears a legend for hunting shirt. This, Hugh certainly did, though the crucial question is whether he came by it honestly or made it himself.

For as it was said of Glass that he beat fiercer odds than those which ambushed any other sampler of frontier potluck, it follows that some today have made a business of doubting what men of his own time did not. If that is a normal occupational hazard for greatness, the motives which impel living men to war upon the long-gone are not uniform.

In some cases the prompting force seems a sheer unwillingness to believe in magnificence. Accordingly Arthur, the patriotic leader, and Bran, the daring mariner, are stabbed by the assertion that they never lived.

Where the fact of the achievement can't be winked away, as in the case of the *Iliad*, the undercutters have squared accounts by taking the poem away from the author known to the Greeks and awarding it to faceless syndicates of round-robin singers. Then there is a country which is not called the United States of Columbia, because some didimus decided that Colombo's won laurels should be given to a man of dubious accomplishments named Amerigo.

A fourth class of tomb defacers are easier to understand than the first three, because the emotions which drive them are of the same order as those which make the fans of one team hostile to the fortunes of another. Shakespeare has been the chief victim of this form of partisanship, as biographers bent on leading cheers for this or that favored character haven't stopped short of robbing the Bard's grave, right down to the last love ditty and bawdy quip, and bestowing the loot elsewhere.

But a dead man can further endanger his good name by taking part in an episode which does not enhance the standing of some other figure, beloved of this or that historian. And it is for this reason that Hugh Glass has been posthumously sandbagged. The details of the offense attributed to him will be presented in their due place, farther on in this chronicle. Here it is enough to say that in the course of the Glass cycle there was an eclipse of Jim Bridger's sun. While some of its many worshipers have been able to retain their liking for Hugh, too, others have been unforgiving.

In their zeal for one great Western character, these have not boggled at trying to annihilate another who had previously enjoyed stardom unchallenged. One highly regarded authority, for example, mustered evidence designed to prove that the episode which jointly featured Glass and Bridger never took place. Nor was J. Cecil Alter (the author of a generally excellent study

of Jim) content with that denial. In order to destroy a
story which had demonstrably been believed by Hugh's
contemporaries, he had to identify the imaginer of
long-current nonsense.

This — and his logic stands up, if his premise can be
granted as sound — he found to be only Glass himself,
dwindled, by that exposure, from epic stature to that
of a buffoon with Bunthorne's "morbid love of admiration." To use Alter's exact term, Hugh was a "Munchau-
sen"; and in summing up his case the prosecutor declared that he would not be for omitting Hugh from all
future works, but merely from ones with any claim to
being historical.

Others, inevitably, have picked up Alter's charge, or
have concluded independently that the Glass cycle was
perhaps a tribute to Hugh's powers of invention. In an
admirable article about William Ashley's role in opening the Overland Trail, for example, Donald McKay
Frost undertook to point out that there was no known
source for Glass's adventures, not counting the man
who said that he had had them.

There is, of course, a hole in that charge which its
framer could only plug by bringing back and cross-
examining all of Hugh's Western acquaintances. Nobody knows who first gave the story oral currency, or
what informants — of whom there were a good few
possible ones, in addition to Hugh — he relied upon
while doing so.

Certainly Glass could have been the only news source
about what went on while he was alone. But there were
witnesses to the events which ended in solitude for him,

while other men saw him at the close of his ordeal. Between them they knew all the salient circumstances, and as rough country veterans, they were able to judge the worth of whatever Hugh might have been called upon to fill in.

No doubt he was "called upon" in the buttonholed sense of being quizzed by fellow trappers probing for the details of his exploit, either out of professional curiosity or to have a tale to tell at coming campfires. In a region of few books (and not too many who could read any that might have been available), the great day's-end amusement was verbal narration.

As long as the era of the wandering Western hunters lasted, Hugh's story was told and believed. But in this of the gasoline-propelled tourist, Glass has been damned as a footless braggart; and the law governing legends reverses the law of the land, in that a man is guilty until proved innocent.

Inquiry with regard to Hugh Glass today must begin with the numerous written references, as well as preserved versions of the central story. These are remarkable for agreeing as to the main points, even though not uniform in the matter of details. The weakness of the defense testimony is that the links between the narrators and the events cannot, in general, be established. In a few cases, though, known mountain men have testified.

Those hostile to, or suspicious of, Glass have made capital out of the fact that a letter-writing trapper named Daniel T. Potts didn't mention Hugh in the course of several letters written between 1826 and 1828, which were published in the *Philadelphia Gazette* at the time. It is now known that the man in question *did* take note of Hugh, in a letter, quoted at the beginning of this discussion, which was written earlier than any of his others.

As to Potts and his significance, more will be said a few pages farther on. Although the first located reference, his report was long buried. It had no bearing on the development of the Glass cycle, whose foundation stone was an item which was also published in a Philadelphia periodical, this time the *Port Folio* of March, 1825.

Run under the department heading LETTERS FROM THE WEST, the article was called "The Missouri Trapper." Reprinted in June of the same year by the *St. Louis Missouri Intelligencer*, it has been the version most leaned upon by subsequent chroniclers. There are, however, no grounds for holding it at all points more authentic than some other versions published later.

Even the name of the author was for long unknown, let alone the identity of a mentioned informant, and the source of the latter's knowledge. After a good few decades had passed, historians began ascribing it to Alphonso Wetmore, author of *Gazeteer of the State of Missouri* and an early report on the Santa Fe Trail. In 1940, though, Randolph C. Randall exploded this theory by publishing in *American Literature* an article called "Authors of the Port Folio Revealed by the Hall Files."

The detective work was made necessary by the low estate of the writing craft in the United States of the nineteenth century's first third. As there were very few professionals, authorship was largely undertaken by men of affairs, who did not wish their colleagues to think that they put undue store by what was, for them, a mere pastime. In consequence, it was the custom to publish work anonymously or over pseudonyms.

Only the directors of a given periodical were supposed to know just who had written what, and during the period which saw the publication of "The Missouri Trapper," the *Port Folio* was owned and run by a discreet pair of publishers, John Elihu Hall and his brother, Harrison. Both went to their graves without betraying any literary confidences; but when Harrison died, it was found that he had noted the authorship of item after item in his set of bound copies of the magazine. Examining these many years later, Mr. Randall was able to assert that the article about Glass was written by James Hall, a young brother of the other two.

Although these had remained in their native Philadelphia, James had gone to the "Western" United States of that day, and in 1825 was a judge in Shawneetown, Illinois. If he had seemingly not been known as a writer up to that time, he became a well established author of books with titles such as *Legends of the West* and *Tales of the Border*. Yet his first book, significantly, was called *Letters from the West*. The earliest version of the Hugh Glass legend was undoubtedly that of James Hall, whose name will be used in referring to it from here on.

But "the West" or even "the Far West" of Hall's day

was more or less settled America, west of the Appalachians but extending no farther toward the Pacific than Missouri. The Great Plains and the Rockies didn't count — not only because they were too distant to have any foothold in most men's ken; they belonged to the United States without being considered a part of it.

The above is worth remarking only to underscore the limits of Hall's personal knowledge of what is now known as the American West, the titles of his books notwithstanding. He was an outsider who somehow learned of Hugh's adventures, and that is the most that can be said.

The next man to write of Glass, though, was one of the great Western figures, albeit without that recognition at the time. Philip St. George Cooke had matriculated at West Point at the tender enough age of fourteen. Four years later, or in 1827, he was given his commission and ordered to report at Jefferson Barracks, near St. Louis.

Subsequently in the West for more than thirty years, he was more familiar with its southern than its northern moiety. Still, he had been stationed at Fort Leavenworth, a post at the gateway to the Upper Missouri region, before he made the first of two contributions to the Hugh Glass cycle. He could thus have talked with men who knew Hugh and his associates. Unluckily, though, he did not name the informants who inspired him to write *Some Incidents in the Life of Hugh Glass, a Hunter of the Missouri*.

Neither, indeed, did he name himself; for he affixed

the *nom de plume* "Borderer" to the work which the *St. Louis Beacon* ran on December 2, and seven days later, in 1830. As in the instance of James Hall, the lieutenant was successful in concealing his authorship, and it wasn't until long afterward that the article was known to be by the same hand as that which wrote *Conquest of New Mexico and California* and — more to the point — *Scenes and Adventures in the Army.*

But many of Cooke's adventures were still ahead of him when a third man undertook to write of Hugh, his bear fight, and its aftermath. Although he had a diplomatic career besides, Edmund Flagg was the first professional author to contribute to the Glass cycle. In his day, which was quite a long one, he was admired alike for his verse, some romantic novels and a historical production or so. Now, though, he is known to few — except Americana fans, who pass his pretentious efforts by in favor of a journalistic stint, called *The Far West.*

Flagg got as far west as eastern Missouri while gathering the material for this work. But he was in St. Louis, among other places; and that city was the fur-trade capital. That's where mountain men went, if they returned to the States at all — and tales of the Upper Missouri and the Rockies were as standard as whiskey in its saloons.

Doubtless the notetaking tourist heard a lot of them, but the one he took home with him was the story of Hugh Glass.

Home in this case was Louisville, Kentucky, where

Flagg was helping George D. Prentice edit the *Louis-ville Literary News Letter*. On September 7, 1839, this periodical published "Adventures at the Headwaters of the Missouri"; and as Flagg was a professional writer, instead of a coy practicer of another trade, he signed it.

Flagg thought he got his data straight from factland. The informant he didn't name (perhaps at the former's request) told the journalist that he had been present when Glass learned how the grizzly bear earned the scientific monicker of *Ursus horribilis*. The fellow couldn't have been all he claimed, for he was hazy as to place relationships, and he got too many names wrong. Only a little wrong, though; and he identified actors whom the others had failed to. He can be classed as a knowledgeable go-between from a primary source to the reporter.

Without giving Flagg's item much more of an audi-ence, the Dubuque, Iowa, *News* reprinted it in Novem-ber of 1839, using the title "History of a Trapper." Playing to a bigger house, an article called "Old Glass" appeared in the *St. Louis Evening Gazette* in March of the ensuing year. Anonymous and allowed to remain so, the only significance of the piece, which added noth-ing to earlier accounts, is that it formed one more proof of the story's hold on readers of the period.

Out on the Great Plains and in the Rockies, mean-while, the tale was still a verbal favorite. Independently, during the 1840's, Rufus Sage and George Ruxton found the story while afield and summarized it in their travel books.

While their reports are too casual to rank as more than supporting parts of the cycle, Cooke published the aforementioned *Scenes and Adventures in the Army*, in 1857. Among other things, the work identified the author of the articles about Glass which had been signed "Borderer" twenty-seven years earlier. Used as stuffing for Cooke's autobiography, they were reprinted almost word for word. A developed form of Hugh's story had thus at last jumped from the dead-letter office of transient periodicals and found a niche between American book covers.

The Civil War, and the changes it boded for the West, caused a long interruption in the evolution of the Glass cycle. The transcontinental railroad, voted as a wartime measure and pressed to conclusion as soon as the fighting was over, reduced the region from a wild outland to a rustic province of a nation with headquarters in the Industrial Age.

Once seen as the only means of making money in the West, the fur trade was vestigial where followed at all. Authors who now wrote of the country dealt with lads involved in stock raising and mining or with bandits who throve on those pursuits, when not raising Cain in the towns inevitably fostered by them. An occasional book harked back to the old days of wilderness free-ranging; but in general they were forgotten, and Hugh Glass along with the rest of the era.

In the last quarter of the nineteenth century, though, the duties of a military engineer named Hiram Martin Chittenden took him into a section which people no longer referred to as "the Upper Missouri." If, else-where, the trappers of the mountains and Plains had been put out of mind, their exploits were still vivid in the memories of the ancient holdovers Chittenden met, whether they were as yet active on the river or waiting for sundown in the settlements, strung along a stream which had once known only trading posts.

What he learned from these speakers for the past urged Chittenden to dig into supporting records. When he had done so, he produced a work which has since sired countless other histories, not to mention a horde of novels and a considerable body of verse. Published in 1902, this literary stud was called *The American Fur Trade of the Far West.*

A compendium of great adventure stories, as well as a history of a commercial epoch, the book brought many an interesting character out of Limbo. Among them was Hugh Glass, of whose exploits the author had learned from an excellent source.

Chittenden's informant was Captain Joseph La Barge, who had gone up the Missouri in 1831, while Hugh was still alive. Although it was not asserted that he had known Glass personally, he certainly had met plenty who did during his many years of service as a trader and steamboat captain up the high Missouri. What he had to say on the subject was what the men with firsthand knowledge had reported; and as La Barge was accounted a man of strict probity, he can be assumed to have made a faithful report of what he had been told.

Chittenden's account, then, is the first to have named

an informant and fixed his relationship, in time and proximity, to Glass and the event which has made Hugh's name a lasting one. In the course of his subsequent research, moreover, the author turned up the *Missouri Intelligencer* reprint of Hall's version. Finding the two accounts in general one, he accepted the story of Hugh Glass as fact, and thus made the drooping legend green again.

One who took note of it was John G. Neihardt, an aspiring writer, whose quest for the stuff of poetry and prose led him first to live with a Plains Indian tribe and then to follow the lead of early fur traders by working a hand-powered boat far up the Missouri. The real old-timers such as La Barge had gone by then, but Neihardt met members of the generation just behind them. These were the sons of the old trappers, traders and river jacks, not of the classic era but close to it in sympathies; and some of its great tales were their own.

They were the last purveyors of oral traditions bearing on the fur trade, some of which were also known to the older Indians of the day. Neihardt listened, as only a writer who senses that he has found a major theme can, and by the time he had put his nonage behind him, he had conceived the ambitious scheme of writing a group of narrative poems about the opening of the West.

The first of these, published in 1915, was *The Song of Hugh Glass*. The worth of this work, considered as a piece of poetry, will not be discussed in this chapter, which is concerned with the fact of many recensions of the Glass legend rather than with their respective literary merits. Suffice it to say, therefore, that the poem presents Hugh's central story in considerable detail, and that it seems to stem from Chittenden's report, supplemented with information which the author took in by ear, while stirring about in the West.

But Neihardt did some independent research, too. He was the first contributor to the Glass cycle to take note of the fact that Hugh had left a piece of writing himself. The document was a letter which Glass had written to the father of a slain comrade. There was no place for it in *The Song of Hugh Glass*, naturally, but Neihardt reproduced it as an illustration of a prose work about the mountain men which he published in 1920 and called *The Splendid Wayfaring*. He drew upon information contained in the note, furthermore, when writing of a famous fur trade episode which earlier had been without explanation.

So Hugh himself was at last heard from, and three years later the first of several men who had unquestionably known him turned in a report. In 1923, that is to say, Charles L. Camp edited for the journal of the California Historical Society the memoirs of George C. Yount.

That simple statement has a complex story behind it, though. The reminiscences of Yount were not jotted down by himself, but were told to an Episcopal clergyman named Clark, whom his parents had undertaken to christen Orange. A Harvard man, with an M.A. won at Columbia, the Reverend Orange Clark had never been in the West until he disembarked from his ship at San Francisco in 1851. At some time during the next few years, he met the former mountain man and decided that his recollections would make an interesting book.

Although he was trivet-right, there were hurdles in the way of proper execution which he didn't know how to jump. He was an amateur, who skimmed over matters of intense interest and was fulsome about ones of less general concern. He obviously didn't know how to draw his subject out, nor did his ignorance of the West and its leading personalities allow him to ask enough of the right questions when Yount proffered a likely topic. Then, although Clark didn't try to give Yount's reminiscences in the first person, he stood between him and the reader as opaquely as does the modern ghost writer, who gives his own jaunty speechways to celebrities who wouldn't know a quip were it labeled in neon. The examiner of his work learns a great deal about how Orange ticked, and parlous little about the insides of the man whose native woodnotes wild he translated into Ivy Leaguese.

Nevertheless, American literature owes the parson a vote of thanks for preserving information, not elsewhere pickled in print, about one of the nation's great legendary figures. For in Clark's rendition of whatever a bred-in-the-bone frontiersman actually said there is the sole account of how Glass reached the West, and what he did there before he turned up as a member of William Ashley's second expedition. His narrative, besides, is one of the two which tell how Hugh wrought

/ 17

between his greatest adventure and his final ones.

A rabbit's-foot was working for the Glass cycle here. Clark's hope of having his manuscript published got a rejection slip from Mrs. Yount, who didn't want the world to know about the rawhide career of a chap who had now become a staked-down man of property. Much of the manuscript was later lost, or possibly scrapped, before Mr. Camp obtained leave to edit it, and much of the rest survived only in the form of the author's notes. But the part dealing with Hugh was handed down intact and fully developed.

It is triply interesting because of cited additional sources. Yount himself did not learn what he knew entirely from Glass, for he drew upon the declared recollections of two other mountain men. Clark didn't have sense enough to note their first names, but their last ones give a line on each. The one called Dutton was mentioned as matched with Hugh in an episode reported by a St. Louis newspaper. The other one, Allen, was reputed to have been with Glass when the latter met the silvertip. As Hugh was surely teamed with a man so surnamed only a few days earlier, that can be believed.

Clark likewise knew this chap, whom he identified as "Allen of Mohave notoriety" — and there dropped him, as though he had written nothing to raise the hair of curiosity. He made it a matter of record, furthermore, that he had palavered about Hugh with Allen, as well as with Dutton, and found that the brain-savings of each checked with the pertinent ones of Yount.

As Dutton and Allen put nothing known in writing,

only Clark and his Sam Johnson remain to be weighed against the document for which they were responsible. The author may be quarreled with, but not on the count of inventing excitement; his butterfingers in handling the balls Yount threw him swear to his innocence. That places the question mark after the man from whom Orange Clark got his data.

Not one of the great mountain men, Yount ranked with the best of the second flight. In California, besides, he won the rating of a notable pioneer.

Yount was west of the Mississippi ahead of most of his trapping associates, for when he was a teenless nipper his family took him from North Carolina to the newly opened Louisiana Purchase, in 1804. Growing up in Missouri's uncombed Girardeau region, he took part in Indian campaigns which included the first against Black Hawk, in 1816. In subsequent years he rose and fell as a stock farmer and rode the Santa Fe Trail in hopes of catching up with his runaway fortunes.

As trapping was the quickest way for a man without capital to make a stake, Yount turned to that trade, after reaching New Mexico in 1825. Hugh Glass was but one of the renowned Westerners with whom he associated in the Southwest. He was with Ewing Young, Milton Sublette, and as yet peg-legless Tom Smith, when these and James Ohio Pattie avenged the massacre of the Michel Robidoux party by the Papagos near the site of Phoenix, Arizona. Following rifle play which made good, if inert, Indians of better than five-score of the murderers, Yount and his companions ranged the Great Basin and the Rockies during much of the rest of 1827.

He probably drank at the mountain-man rendezvous of that year, and certainly did at those of the following two. At the second of these he met Jed Smith, with whose accounts of California he was greatly impressed. Deciding to go there himself, he accompanied William Wolfskill, when, in 1830, the latter opened the Old Spanish Trail from Santa Fe to the Coast. Or maybe he helped reopen it, as some historians believe the Old Spaniards had once used it themselves.

Beyond the Sierras, Yount became, among other things, a catcher of sea otter. In this pursuit he was the tutor of George Nidever, a buckskin who wrote his own account of experiences that also included membership in the party which Bonneville sent to California in 1833, with Joe Walker in command. Nor are Nidever's the only memoirs of a mountain man which mention Yount. He was a known and respected member of a craft from which he retired, as of 1836, to become the first settler of Napa Valley. Arriving five years ahead of his nearest competitor, he held on in the face of Indian attacks and achieved the prosperity which had long eluded him.

By all accounts it was an earned prosperity, attained by a man who was considered nothing of a boaster. Neither can it be said that he puffed his own exploits in the report of them he gave to Orange Clark. Yount, in sum, was honest, as well as informed on mountain-man matters, and there is no reason to believe that he would turn mythmaker when speaking of Glass.

Clearing Yount of duplicity is not the same thing, of

course, as establishing the truthfulness of Hugh. Yet, in judging him, the sophistication of the colleagues who believed in him must be weighed. These were not greenhorns for any horn tooter to impose upon, but the hard-case professionals of an exceedingly rough trade.

When knowing buckers of the same falls single out one of their fellows as the champion salmon, he is unlikely to prove no more than a blowfish. And the voice of Western consensus was speaking when Yount gave Clark a general appraisal of Hugh Glass which the minister reworded as follows: "In point of adventures, dangers and narrow escapes and capacity for endurance, and the sufferings which befel him, this man was preeminent."

In 1928 Charles L. Camp edited the memoirs of another old-timer, in this case one who had gone up the Missouri with Ashley when Hugh did so. James Clyman had been a member of the party which Jed Smith had led through South Pass in 1824, and something of Hugh's genius for finding hot water to plunge into had made him a celebrated figure.

So there was no doubt as to the worth of his testimony, but in the case of Glass it was so brief as to have been something Tacitus might have written when cramped for space. No more than reporting that Hugh and a grizzly had had a tussle, Clyman said nothing at all about the dramatic aftermath. That omission on the part of such an informant greatly cheered the anti-Glass faction among historians, who chose to ignore the fact that James was chiefly concerned with his own experiences — and not those of Hugh or anybody else, when he had no part in them.

So Clyman's failure to mention that Glass had survived abandonment was taken by some as just grounds for declaring the whole episode had never taken place outside of Hugh's imagination. For, as they were able to point out then, neither was it mentioned by Daniel T. Potts, the letter-writing mountain man.

This seemed a very telling point, because Potts was an inmate of the post toward which Glass was heading at the time of the asserted bear encounter. He was also a member of the party which Hugh was said to have joined following recovery from his wounds. Yet letters of his which cited contemporary events had made no mention of an event calculated to draw a comment from his pen.

Of the two, only the Hugh Glass story was on trial, for there was no doubt as to the authenticity of the letters. Potts was a Pennsylvanian who had got tired of running a mill in Montgomery County and had gone West in time to join Ashley's expedition of 1822. It was several years before he got around to writing to a brother living in Philadelphia, but, as the latter turned them over to the *Philadelphia Gazette*, they were available to historians, who found them to be the earliest reports in certain instances. Potts, for example, was the first to write an account of the natural wonders of the Yellowstone Lake area.

The fact that he did so proved of service to the Hugh Glass saga. For as Potts was, so to speak, the godfather of Yellowstone Park, the custodians of its museum were delighted to receive, from the mountain man's grandnieces, overtures which led to the purchase of the famous letters, together with a copy of one whose contents had never been made public. Written earlier than any of the others, it was found to contain a neat summation of Hugh's bear fight and the events that followed.

Glass was not named, but there was no reason why Potts should have identified him when writing to Thomas Cochlen of Cheltenham, Pennsylvania. It was enough that he authored a communication which got down to business as follows:

After leaving you I arrived in Illanois in July the same year and tarried there until mid winter and from thence to Masuri where I tarried until spring from there I embarked for the Rocky Mountains and the Columbia for the purpose of hunting and traping and trading with the Indians in a company of about on hundried men. We hoisted our sails on the third day of April 1822 at Saint Lewis . . .

Headed *Rocky Mountains, July 7, 1824*, the missive is remarkable because of the style, as compared with that which the *Philadelphia Gazette* had taught investigators to expect of the writer. But it, and not the ones previously published over the signature of Potts, represented his true literary level.

The originals of the known letters, complete with jottings by another hand, showed that deletions, as well as editorial doctoring, had bastardized the texts of what the historians of a century and more had thought to be the straight testimony of a primary Western observer. Matched against the items which their author had actually produced, they turned out to be very poor relations. If no one whom grammarians would take as a model, Daniel Potts had tossed off passages which crackled with personality. Or they did, until they had been sucked bare of blood by some vampire of an editor, who had reduced them to standardization and left them with as little life as was left to Hugh by the silvertip.

Owning valuable documents, the Park's curators did their best to make them a matter of common knowledge by publishing them in a 1947 issue of *Yellowstone Nature Notes*. But as this periodical was read by fans of natural rather than human history, professionals in the latter field missed its message to them. In consequence the anchoring passage of the Hugh Glass cycle was overlooked, and chroniclers who cited Hugh continued to write as though it had never been discovered.

That condition lasted for a decade. In 1957, though, Aubrey L. Haines, Yellowstone Park's historian, contributed an article to a symposium titled *Historical Essays on Montana and the Northwest*. In his part of the potpourri, Mr. Haines at last made Western Americana wranglers aware of what Potts had written about Hugh.

Seven years earlier, in his biography of Jed Smith, Dale Morgan had performed the same service with regard to an item which his enterprise had brought to light. This was a letter which a frontiersman named Sanford had written to William Clark in 1833. In one of its passages, the death of Glass was dealt with.

Although others may be dredged up at any time,

those are the known American sources. A couple of foreign ones, both German, remain to be considered.

Between 1832 and 1834 Alexander Philip Maximilian, Prince of Wied, had Western experiences which he told about in a work of several volumes published in Coblentz as they slid off his pen between 1839 and 1841. In 1843, this travelogue was published in London under the title *Travels in the Interior of North America*. An American edition did not appear until 1906, when Reuben Gold Thwaites issued it in three annotated installments.

Arriving at Hugh's final stamping ground not many months after Glass went under, Prince Maximilian knew of him through close associates. Unluckily, however, he took note only of Hugh's passing and what was done about it.

The other German production which features Glass is a curiosity of literature. Never Englished in full, it is a little-known contribution to the lore of the West called *Lebensbilder aus den Vereinigten Staaten von Nordamerika und Texas*. Written by Friederich Wilhelm von Wrede and published in Cassel, Germany, in 1844, it covered the author's American experiences, beginning with his arrival in New Orleans in 1836.

It is not necessary to name the scholars posthumously hoaxed by this countryman of Baron Munchhausen only a few years ago. Suffice it to say that they examined his work and were gratified to learn that von Wrede had, in 1844, published a Hugh Glass narrative which worked out in English as just about a word-for-word rendering of what Philip St. George Cooke had published thirteen years later in *Scenes and Adventures in the Army*. Cooke was then accused, in print, of lifting and claiming as his own a version of Hugh's story which had in fact been composed by a German, whose work he had somehow run across.

The charge is nullified by comparing both with the little-examined parent account, signed "Borderer" and published in 1830. The style is Cooke's. He was not the plagiarizer; the real claim-jumper was a foreigner who had happened to encounter Cooke's old newspaper articles and decided to use them.

But the strange history of this version doesn't stop there. A sufficient wealth of evidence shows that the fatal winter for Hugh was that of 1832-1833, while von Wrede, as has been pointed out, did not set foot in the United States until several years later. Yet he undertook to declare that the source of his stolen account was none other than Glass himself.

What makes this queer business odder still is that the episode is said, by those at ease in German, to be the March hare of an otherwise soberly factual book. The author's purpose was to produce a work which would tell Teutons who might be considering America as a home just what the raw immigrant could expect to find west of the Atlantic. But spang in the middle of this guidebook, he stuck Hugh's fetch — a garrulous spirit who gave a man with an indifferent store of English a complexly worded story of his life.

The circumstances of this unusual interview were these:

The German stayed in New Orleans long enough to be able to gain a certain fluency in the language of the States and Texas. Faring up the Mississippi, in May of 1836 he was on a packet which stopped at Hopefield, Arkansas. Since engulfed by the Father of Waters, it was then directly across the river from Memphis.

On the landing at Hopefield stood a man in buckskin, carrying a rifle and the other instruments of a wandering hunter's trade. Aboard the steamer, he turned out to be Hugh Glass, fresh from the Western wilds.

Charity can, to be sure, suppose certain extenuating possibilities. The fact of Hugh's death may not have been generally known in the Mississippi Valley, though Flagg picked up news of it there not too much later. It can also be postulated that von Wrede was spotted for a mark by a frontiersman who deemed it no more than fair to please with a good story a greenhorn willing to set up the drinks.

As Hugh Glass was about the only Westerner whose name was known to those from other parts, the German could have paved the way for what followed by asking the borderer if he knew the man who'd met a bear. The German could then have gained an earful, from a chap whose racy dialect a foreigner couldn't reproduce; so he had therefore substituted Cooke's report of what, to von Wrede, was a memorable occasion.

But as he didn't say that last, he must stand the judgment of percentage. It's barely possible that he could have been innocent of all but the hit-and-run charge of unconfessed cribbing. The odds, however, put him down as an unmitigated fraud.

It has the look, too, of an unmotivated fraud; but the fact that there's no such thing is what gives significance to this odd chapter of the Hugh Glass cycle. Under whatever circumstances, there can only have been one reason for the inclusion of Hugh's history in a work never designed to hold it, and that is the fascination of the material.

The tale called as persuasively to an alien, fresh from Europe, as it did to the native-born residents of American towns and Hugh's own colleagues of the distant West. It is the most primal story — far more so than any preserved by the writings of far more ancient peoples — to be found anywhere in literature. For that cause is it as new as it was yesterday, or will be tomorrow.

If it is extant in versions which don't fully agree, that is also true of current events, as reported by different newspapers and reviewed by rival columnists. But in this case the competitive accounts have never been compared and sifted for probabilities. Doing that will be one of the occupations of the rest of this work. Otherwise it will be devoted to weaving one story out of Hugh's accredited exploits, and expounding the events which set the stage for them.

PART I

∧∧∧∧∧∧∧∧∧∧∧

The Buildup by History

I

/\/\/\/\/\/\

The Initiation of a Westerner

*Glass first commenced life in the capacity of a
sailor; and after having followed the seas during
several years, was captured by the desperate band of
Pirates under the notorious Lafitte.*
— CLARK'S RECORDING OF YOUNT'S REMINISCENCES

THE FIRST English-speaking white man to acquire
legendary stature wholly in the West emerged
from the sea in middle life, leaving his former years,
and all that must have befallen a born adventurer in
the course of them, blanketed in mist. One wisp of tradition, as bare of a roosting place as any other chicken
of Mother Carey, has it that Hugh Glass hailed from
Pennsylvania. When he did, or whereabouts in the Keystone State, are matters on which even folklore has
nothing to declare.

Glass did, it is known, confide in one biographer, but
the work turned out by the latter was never published
and cannot now be located. Tantalizingly, it was described in an item which did get printed. Prince Maximilian of Wied noted that its author read the piece to
him and that it made good hearing.

If the manuscript is ever found, it may reveal much about Hugh's background, though quite possibly it might not. As even George Yount seems to have known nothing of his friend's pre-Western career, it is reasonable to wonder if Hugh told any fellow frontiersman what he had done before he met another seafaring man, also with a past which none has been able to trace.

Some annalists have called Jean Lafitte a Creole, or white native of French and Spanish possessions in the New World. Others have averred that he was born in this or that city along the coast of France proper. Some have guessed that he was born about 1780, while others have preferred not to risk a date. All that is known is that French was his native tongue and that he was a man of full maturity when he and his elder brother, Pierre, turned up in New Orleans about 1809.

As to where he might have been before, there is only the testimony of a secretive man, not above lying for his own amusement, as well as for the solider purpose of hiding his connection with criminal actions. For what it is worth, then, Lafitte told a group of United States Naval officers that he had once prospered as a merchant in Santo Domingo, then a French holding, where he had also been the devoted husband of a Creole beauty. But this idyllic state of affairs came to an end when a Spanish man-cf-war seized a vessel on which Jean was voyaging, and marooned him and his bride on a deserted key. Although at length rescued by American mariners, Madame Lafitte did not long survive the brutal experience, which was the one to which Jean attributed his yen for scuttling Spanish ships.

Jean was able to carry off such a tale, for he was in all things — save the viciousness which told him how to thrive as a criminal — the romantic novelist's rogue. When he chose to, he bore himself like a man of culture, and a courtly one withal. Ashore he flashed a dandy's wardrobe, and was a gourmet who loved to display his knowledge of fine drinkables. There were rumors, perhaps started by himself, that other duelists had found him rarely apt with a rapier. And then, of course, there was his unexceptionable conduct at the Battle of New Orleans.

Yet ashore, too, Lafitte was that peculiarly mean figure, the passer of stolen goods acquired through risks taken by others. It was in this capacity that he first gained a foothold in history. For by 1810 it had come to be understood, by those who knew the inner workings of New Orleans, that Jean and Pierre Lafitte were not merely the owners of the blacksmith shop they had opened on St. Philip Street but were black ivory dealers as well. They were, indeed, fences for the smugglers of Barataria, whose contraband included job lots of Negro slaves.

Whether tide-besieged Barataria was named for the isle of which Sancho Panza was dubbed governor, or whether it was so named because its dwellers stoned the marine penal code, has been a disputed matter. But whatever the truth there, the area's shoal waters and islands bristling with palmettos had long made up a region where maritime rogues were as common as fiddler crabs.

Insofar as is known, they had not earlier been organized, at least on any general scale. The brothers Lafitte presiding, though, they joined forces and grew in criminal stature until they were no longer seen as mere duty evaders and barrators of coastal craft, but were recognized as pirates of the high seas, willing and able to attack merchantmen of any size.

Or rather, molding the Baratarians into a band of buccaneers seems to have been Jean's work, while Pierre was the business genius of the outfit. When they were in full career, in sum, the latter was the chief of operations who planned strategy ashore, while his brother became the naval commander who did the actual fighting. It was thus never Pierre who was meant by "Lafitte the Pirate," but Jean.

According to his own account, Jean had practiced marine ravin while in the West Indies. Before the end of 1810, in any case, he taught the coastal toughs of Louisiana the techniques of buccaneering, which he had learned somewhere. Within a few years, so effective was his tutelage, he had formed an organization which did more than blight the health of New Orleans as a seaport. It threatened the welfare of all Trans-Appalachia, whose produce flowed down its numberless river roads, alike in leading to the Crescent City.

There were those in the afflicted region who favored a sure cure. Andrew Jackson, for example, voiced a wish to admire Jean Lafitte in the act of being hanged. Yet for once Old Hickory had to take one of his calls for gore back. The same War of 1812 which had kept the United States Navy too busy to attend to that of Barataria drew Jackson to New Orleans at the head of an army without the artillery needed to ward off the better armed military invasion which Great Britain was mounting. But the pirate had, and didn't hold back, the big guns, and the men trained to use them, which the General lacked.

For this occasion, besides, Lafitte had so far stepped out of his normally venal character that he had spurned a British offer of pay, if he would support the force led by the Duke of Wellington's brother-in-law, Lieutenant General Edward Pakenham. What the lord of Barataria put at Old Hickory's disposal was, on the other hand, proffered free of charge; and Jean himself skippered a vessel whose mission was that of scouting the ships of the Royal Navy. These were working their way up the Mississippi as part of a land and sea assault which would have been successful but for the picaroons of the Gulf.

Those of them who manned the cannon they had brought ashore were deft at scoring with them, fired in tune to the pitch and roll of ships afloat. Aiming from firm emplacements, they displayed a marksmanship to match the rifles of the frontier hunters who made up the body of Jackson's force. Veterans of the Napoleonic wars though they were, the British had never been up against such a deadly combination. Neither before nor since, it can be affirmed, has an English army been beaten so badly by a force which gave away odds of better than two to one.

Jackson was pleased, as he had reason to be; and his report of Lafitte's conduct transformed Jean from a despised rascal into a national hero. As James Madison added the whitewash of a Presidential pardon for all past breaches of the law, its receiver was free to capitalize on his fine gesture by stepping on the WELCOME mat placed for his use by upright society. But as Byron pointed out in *The Corsair*, Lafitte had exhausted his stock of nobility by that one display, while as a villain he was a career man. So after the celebrations in his honor had given way to normal, rack-along living, Jean grew bored with good citizenship and put to sea as a freebooter again.

He didn't straightway lose favor with Americans by backsliding, for his story was that he had merely resumed his old custom of attacking Spanish ships. Spain had always been a bothersome neighbor of the United States, because of a colonial policy which funneled all the exports of her possessions in the New World through the mother country. In consequence, American merchants had been denied trade with Mexico and, while it had remained in Spanish hands, fur-rich Upper Louisiana. At that period, too, New Orleans had been closed to American shipping from time to time. And if these were solved problems, the hostile attitude of Spain, with regard to Mexican commerce, remained. Then, keeping company with it, were the Texas and Florida questions.

The colonial officials in charge of Florida had proved unable to control bands of Indians and fugitive Negroes, which periodically raided Georgia. The situation with respect to Texas was no less irritating, although here the bad blood welled from a sore made by Napoleon, rather than by the royal government of Spain. In selling both Louisianas to America, Bonaparte had tossed in Texas, where Spanish settlements had replaced long defunct French ones. Further to complicate matters, the Texas of Gallic notions stretched as far as the northward swing of the Rio Grande, thus raking in towns belonging to the separate province of New Mexico. The Louisiana Purchase had, of course, been made with French maps for warrant. The United States had thought itself the possessor of all they showed to be for sale, and was not happy about the prior claims to southwestern parts which Spain was able to put forward.

So if he had been forced to abandon his plan to invade North America, the Little Corporal had done the next best thing in the way of causing trouble, by throwing the above-described bone across the Atlantic for the dogs of war to growl over. As it had officially bought Texas, America was determined not to give it up without compensation. Having long administered the region as part of Mexico, Spain saw no reason to recognize the sale, especially after Waterloo left the seller without a voice in international affairs.

So Lafitte made no enemies in America by announcing that he would continue his private feud with Spain. Neither did he, at first, cause anything but grins of satisfaction when he chose a point in the disputed territory for his base of operations.

Where Jean had anchored his fleet in 1815 and the following year is another of the blank spots in his biography. He had not, of course, returned to Barataria, for the United States had emerged from a war of few rewards as a naval power with the guns to keep pirates out of its waters. Perhaps he had tried the West Indies once more; but the Caribbean was not the roadstead for picaroons that it had been during the years in which so many ships of the British Navy had been engaged in blockading Napoleon's European empire. But, to move from speculation to fact, Jean picked a known naval station in 1817, and in so doing he became the founder of a Western town.

The site Jean Lafitte chose for his headquarters was exactly that of the modern city of Galveston, which is located at the eastern end of the island so named. This in turn rides partly athwart the throat of the great Texas bay which is likewise named for Bernardo de Galvez. Lafitte's town, though, did not swell the chorus of tributes to an otherwise-forgotten governor of Spanish Louisiana. Jean called it Campeachy.

Aside from having an excellent harbor, facing toward the mainland, Campeachy offered Lafitte the diplomatic shelter he needed. Claiming Texas, the United States would have used its navy to see to it that no buccaneer used American territory as a base. But from this normal course the Federal government was turned by an unwillingness to provoke the rival claimant. For although Lafitte's attacks were ruinously destructive to Spanish shipping in the Gulf, Madrid told Washington not to interfere with the transplanted Baratarians.

The reason for this action was sound enough. By granting the United States jurisdictional powers, Spain would have gone far toward recognizing American ownership of Texas. So if the fading Spanish Empire did not have the might to cope with the pirates of Galveston Island, it blocked action by the nation which could have handled the matter; and, as American merchantmen were supposedly not being molested, the United States didn't press the matter.

Allowed to thrive, Campeachy did so after a malign fashion whose nearest American match was Natchez Underhill. But that cockroach hive was not sovereign; it was a slum of handsome Natchez on the Bluff. The scum of Campeachy, male and female, were also its first citizens and social arbiters.

Lafitte arrived with rogues and their drabs to the number of eight hundred, white, black and all the intervening hues made possible by the mixture of these with each other, as well as the sundry shades of red native to a variety of Indian tribes. Needing no more in a mild climate, they housed themselves in tents made of sails, or in cabins which were rarely more than lean-tos and wickiups; and their places of trade were equally flimsy. The only solid structures in the town were a small fort, whose battery of four cannon guarded the entrance to the harbor, and a large mansion. In the latter's top story there were also big guns, pointed seaward. On the two lower floors were the lavishly furnished quarters of Jean and his quadroon mistress. Suitably blood-colored, this gubernatorial residence was known as La Maison Rouge.

From this command post Lafitte deployed his flotilla along the traffic lanes of the Gulf of Mexico. The vessels returned laden with both supplies for home consumption and items which could be fenced off either to smugglers or to honest Johns who paid duty in the cheerful knowledge that they had more than saved the cost by buying at Jean's cut-rate market.

The ships serving this market brought in living as well as inanimate items. They brought in Negroes hijacked from slavers. They brought from captured craft the crews and passengers who hadn't been killed during the struggle for possession, or murdered as useless later. At length and after this fashion, one of Lafitte's homing vessels made a Westerner out of Hugh Glass.

Although the theory that the hero of New Orleans preyed on Spanish merchantmen only was one which Americans were anxious to believe, it was a notion canceled by long-hidden facts. In those days of wooden, wind-powered ships and unharnessed airwaves, the mortality of oceangoing vessels was high, and the means of finding what had become of them nil. When a craft didn't return there was grief in related family quarters and resignation in commercial ones; but such disappearances were of too common occurrence to cause more than the comments of heartbreak and disappointment.

Nor was piracy, on the strength of the odds, the first suspect. The sea itself was recognized as the great killer of seamen; they died when it and abetting winds bowled over their ships, or wrenched them apart, or flung them on rocks and reefs, there to be hammered to pieces. Those things happened all the time, and were viewed as the normal hazards of a trade which nobody thought of as a friend to longevity.

So, unless someone escaped to tell of pursuit and attack by men who looked only to the Jolly Roger for authority to wage war, nobody suspected Lafitte — who in turn saw to it that none got away to be talkative. How many non-Spanish ships his own plundered and sank before one of his crew slipped and gave the game away, only the account books of Davy Jones would show. But that Jean was an all-around pirate as early as 1817, or thereabouts, is shown by what Hugh Glass told George Yount.

Which of Jean's lieutenants took the craft which had brought Hugh to the Gulf, from a nameless home port, cannot be told; Yount's recorder left blanks in those spots. But in any case, up went the black flag of ill omen, and buccaneers boarded another victim.

In all likelihood this was an American ship, its commander, Captain Glass. He was literate at a period when men before the mast were rarely so. In middle life, he was of an age to be master, granting that he had the force of character. And of this commodity he was nowise short. It was noticed of him, furthermore, that he had a bent for solitude, a quirk common to sea captains, because of the tradition which held them aloof from companionship while under sail.

Physically, he was a tall man, put together to last. That could be said in triplicate of his spirit, which was as enduring and undaunted by rigors as was ever that of the wandering King of Ithaca. As for his mind, it was attested to have been alert and well informed, while in nature he was held likable and a man to tie to in spite of the independence which made him often prefer his own company, when on the march in mountains or prairies.

His age can be guessed with as little confidence as in the case of Lafitte's. Some years later fellow trappers were wont to refer to him as "Old Glass"; but they were in their twenties for the most part, and inclined to look upon any of a maturer vintage as overripe. In all likelihood their view of elderliness was no more to be relied on than is that of today's suckling soldiers, who hail as "Pop" any comrade who has outlasted his thirtieth birthday.

A fair estimate would seem to be that Hugh was in his middle thirties when his buccaneer captors arranged to see to it that none told. This was not entirely accomplished by murder, for Jean was still enlarging his organization. So, after taking each prize, the pirates gave those of its crew who looked hardy enough to be worth recruiting a chance to "jine" a gang which they had just learned that they couldn't "lick."

Those who refused this offer were slain, or were tossed overboard, to float until they sank. Already dead or floundering hopelessly in the water, of course, were the seamen and male passengers not viewed as picaroon timber. As to what befell any women, it is only necessary to say that the buccaneers of Galveston Island did not share the innate chivalry of the Pirates of Penzance.

Yet, unlike such luckless draftees of Campeachy (of whom none was probably present, as feminine travelers were rare in the Gulf), Hugh was given a choice as to what he would do. The coin handed him was one with two bad sides, but in after years he was to prove, as few in history have done, the truth of the aphorism "While there's life there's hope." Tenacious of his vital spark as the Phoenix, he would not throw it away. Trusting to his resourcefulness to get him out of a bag he fancied as little as any other man of clean instincts, he agreed to become one of Jean Lafitte's picaroons.

As Glass implied to George Yount, the reality of being a pirate far topped in horror any vision of the trade possible to one who hadn't been enmeshed in it. This can be well believed, being akin to the unpreparedness of healthy eyes for the astigmatic one of the narcotic serf. There are monstrosities of conduct belonging to a society which has cut itself off from honor and compassion that outsiders can only understand at the price of forced association.

Thus Hugh found himself on the wrong team when corruption came, saw and conquered. Nor was escape as feasible as it would have been had Lafitte's freebooters been elsewhere-based.

Campeachy was hardly second to Devil's Island in the difficulties it put in the way of any who might wish to leave it in secret. It is true that other than pirate ships made it a port of call. Merchantmen came from as far away as Philadelphia, New York and Boston, lured by the throw-away prices Jean could post, even w' 'e allowing himself a generous markup above the cost of obtaining them. It is alike true that free-lance slave runners — Jim Bowie of the knife was one — plied back and forth between Louisiana and Campeachy. But although Northern buyers of stolen goods and Southern smugglers of human contraband could and did tell themselves that it was all right to deal with the man who had helped Andy Jackson at New Orleans, they despised the lesser buccaneer fry, and would as soon have invited the company of a yellow fever case as to have helped one of them to return to the States.

Many years short of being counted among these, Texas was an all but pathless wilderness. Although there were a few Spanish settlements, none of Hugh's raffish associates knew or cared about the region's geography. Lafitte could have enlightened Glass, to be sure. Through some snake twist of bureaucracy, the scourge of New Spain's commerce was on the payroll of its officials in the capacity of a spy upon American and British moves with regard to Texas. But Jean had no intention of telling any of the flies in his web how they might get out.

In this connection, too, Lafitte could count upon a fact about the disputed province which *was* generally known to his followers. The mainland on both sides of Galveston Bay was infested with Karankawa Indians, hearty cannibals all.

This had been learned at the expense of men who didn't live to profit by the lesson. Crossing the channel to hunt for otherwise unprocurable fresh meat, they found, and tried to abduct, a squaw. They were so far from being able to do this, according to the complaint of a lone survivor, that from three to five of them (as usual in matters pertaining to the West, there are variant versions), stayed to furnish potluck for her, among other pleased redskins.

Not many North American tribes were given to cannibalism, and for most of these the eating of human flesh was a rarely sanctioned ceremonial matter, or was indulged in because of a belief in the benefits to be thereby gained. For instance, the Tonkawas, also of Texas, ate only the hands and feet of enemy warriors slain in battle. The reason for an act, comparable to eating the neck of a chicken and discarding the breast and drumsticks, was the faith that the consumer would add the dead man's manual strength and speed of foot to his own physical arsenal.

But the Karankawas, as they were to prove time and again before the Texas Rangers were formed for the express purpose of ruining their appetites, downright loved long pig for itself alone. Doubtless the residents of Campeachy had heard of grisly banquets other than the one but now cited. And thus the people, thus the fauna of their habitat — which abounded in coral snakes, copperheads, cottonmouths, rattlers and alligators.

The day came, nonetheless, when Hugh looked toward this fearsomely animate shore as his sole hope. Just what had taken place Yount, if he knew, didn't choose to tell the Reverend Orange Clark; but the latter noted that a certain piratical chore had at last so revolted Glass and an unnamed wearer of the same ill-fitting boots that they mutinied and refused to take part. As a result they were told what they already knew, that they were not the stuff of buccaneers. Fortunately for them, though, the man of La Maison Rouge didn't delegate the right to pass sentence on hands that had failed him, so the pair went unpunished, pending a hearing before Lafitte following the return to Campeachy from wherever at sea their captain logged them as having gone on strike.

How long Hugh had served as a pirate in good standing is one of the many interesting bits of information which Clark might well have been in position to pass along but did not. As he did, however, imply that Hugh was the witness of numberless acts of Jolly Roger depravity, it can be inferred that Glass was a freebooter for a year or better.

The only guide lines here are dates bearing principally on other matters. Lafitte was said to have taken over Galveston Island in the first half of 1817, and he was already there when Hugh was captured. But although Jean remained at Campeachy until 1820, there is an intervening date to be reckoned with. In June of 1819 James Long led a band of American frontiersmen into Texas and took over the Spanish outpost town of Nacogdoches, itself not very many leagues from Louisiana. Knowledge of this was not long in reaching Galveston Island, for Long decided to make Lafitte's flotilla the naval arm of the Republic he proclaimed. There was thus open communication between the two Texas communities, as opposed to the secretiveness which had marked Jean's dealings with Spanish officials.

Had Hugh's defection as a pirate taken place after the middle of 1819, then, he would have known in a general way where Nacogdoches was, and so had the bearings he remained without. Such being the case, his mutiny probably put him in deep trouble during the latter part of 1818, or in the early months of the following year.

Having no doubts as to what Jean would decide to do with them, Glass and his comrade agreed not to wait for the pirate chief to tell them about it. They were free to act, because it was reasoned that they could do nothing but stay aboard, when their ship dropped its anchor and the rest of the crew rowed ashore for the carouse with which disaster for others was customarily celebrated. The two apostate picaroons were thus neither confined nor in irons when left to themselves — a circumstance due to the lack of discipline among rogues rather than to luck. At sea, the freebooters might respond to commands smartly enough; but, once a voyage was over, none would consent to be left out of the booze fighting and whoring which awaited them on land.

Meanwhile, Hugh and his partner prepared to risk what men in less desperate straits thought they would not, and that night they dropped over the side. With two miles to swim and littoral currents to buck, the luggage of the fugitives had to be scant. Yount stated that they had the foresight to take along some items of trade. Not that they hoped to be able to keep outside of any encountered Karankawas; this was done in the trust that they would live to meet Indians with whom it was possible to be less intimate.

Although Yount mentioned nothing else, a knife apiece, flint and steel, plus a little food and the minimum essentials of clothing must have burdened the swimmers. As their captors would not have left them firearms, they were relieved of the temptation to try to carry pistols, shot and a waterproof powder container. Neither is it likely that their gear included anything as hard to drag through the water as shoes. Pitifully small as their stock of accouterments was, however, Glass was to look back on the days which found him possessed of his share of them as a period of comparative prosperity.

At the western end of their swim, the truant pirates struggled ashore on the southern side of Galveston Bay. Apart from cannibals, caymans and venom-laden snakes, the hazards of the region embraced cane jungles of excruciating thickness, and bayous whose bottoms were quagmires.

The hordes of reptiles and amphibia to be found there made it easy for the fugitives to keep supplied with nourishment as long as they remained in the low country near the sea — for even the poisonous snakes were good to eat. This was healthy food, that is to say — if not in all cases items to cheer gourmets. It was after they left the rank, coastal rim behind that their survival powers were first really tested.

Granted knowledge of the region, their ordeal need not have been a long one. By following the coast down to the San Antonio River and ascending that stream, they could have reached the Spanish garrison town of La Bahia (now Goliad) in something like a week. But Spanish secrecy with regard to the Empire's possessions had kept most Americans from having any but a very general idea as to how the land lay in the vast territory which Napoleon had tossed in as makeweight for the Louisiana Purchase proper. Such maps as existed were not readily obtainable. So it is not surprising that Hugh — accustomed, as a mariner, to think of even well-settled countries in terms of their seaports — was as ignorant concerning the interior of a half-legendary zone as he owned to Yount that he was.

He and the other did know, of course, that the States they were anxious to reach had a shore which merged with that of Texas — but they knew about the Karankawas, too. Anxious to get clear of these man-eaters as soon as possible, they cut away from the coast into the prairie Plains, a region whose unobtrusive landmarks gave strangers nothing as an aid to holding a course. There was the sun, to be sure, and, had they been afloat, the mariners would have no doubt made a better business of steering by it. In the unfamiliar world of high grass and the groves which dotted it, they angled westerly instead of bearing to the east, as they left the south behind.

In working their way north, they must have been within a day's march of Nacogdoches, or a couple at the most. It might be asked why they did not follow the trace, connecting this Spanish town with the larger one then known as San Fernando de Bexar, though since called San Antonio. Such a duct did exist, even though traffic along it was a rare event. But when it is recalled that the great Santa Fe Trail was at points so scratched-out by migrating buffalo herds that even veteran Westerners couldn't keep from straying, it is not strange that two unaccustomed wanderers should have crossed a little-used pathway without guessing that they had done so.

But, if lost, they were leaving tenderfoot days behind with a rapidity possible only to men who must learn or die. They were, it can be said without belittling their achievement, lucky in the place they went to school. The Texas of that day boasted game (with wild cattle swelling the count) in unrivaled profusion. Even the canniest of hunters can't outwit absent game; but tyros with the gumption to keep at it can get their cut of abundance on the wing, even though armed only with bows of unseasoned wood, or such dawn-man weapons as stones and throwing sticks.

So it is not wonderful that they were after some fashion able to live off the country. What is amazing is that they were able to get as far as they did without meeting Indians looking for scalps to flaunt at some tribal merriment. At least it is astonishing until Cabeza de Vaca's sixteenth-century jaunt from Florida to Mexico is borne in mind.

Their very destitution was of some help in this respect. Lacking rifles and horses, Glass and his fellow had nothing which made them of interest to the bands of warrior thieves they must have at times encountered. Still, Indians were apt to welcome any opportunity to lift hair — that of women and children being as welcome as any other, when they were in the mood. Especially dangerous to ill-armed strays were young bucks eager to prove themselves, chiefs anxious to supply the wherewithal of a scalp dance, or a disappointed war party on the lookout for any face-saving prize. But as the stranded seamen didn't meet any of these, they pressed doggedly up the wrong side of north.

In the course of their journey, they went through the realm of the foot-and-hand-gnawing Tonkawas, as well as that of the torso-guzzling Karankawas. They passed through the hunting grounds of the Osages, who prized a victim's whole head in place of a mere patch of hair. They passed through districts ranged by such avid scalp harvesters as the Comanches and Kiowas. Yet their luck didn't fly away until, roughly a thousand miles from their starting point, they were scooped up, in what is now Kansas, by a band of Pawnees.

Different tribal legends assert that this Indian people had come to the central Great Plains from the Southeast and the Southwest. In any case they had developed a culture which was a cross between that of true town dwellers like the Zuñis, say, and the life pattern of such nomadic tepee-toters as the Blackfeet. In the winter and through spring planting time the Pawnees lived in lodges of logs and earth, each of them big enough to house several families. The rest of the year, aside from the period devoted to harvesting their corn, beans and pumpkins, they joined the peoples who looked to wild animal and bird life for their sustenance.

The staple item, of course, was the buffalo, and the bison stamping ground which the Pawnees regarded as their own preserve was western Kansas. Thither all four groups of them trooped seasonally south from their villages in Nebraska river valleys. The Grand, the Tappage and the Republican Pawnees — who owed their designation to a river and not to fealty to the politics now symbolized by the elephant — do not seem to have had any customs which made one distinguishable from others, as far as outsiders were concerned. But the suitably named Pawnee Loups, or Wolf Pawnees, were given to human sacrifice, both for the purposes of pleasing tribal gods and for pyromancy. The latter practice called for using human ashes as tea leaves, in order to read the future.

A favored ceremony of these Pawnees was the burning of a young girl as a tribute to the planet Venus in its capacity as the Morning Star. It seems probable, on the strength of preserved tribal lore, that originally the sacrificed maidens were Pawnees, dedicated by families with the same eye for the hereafter which made Abraham willing to gain grace by cutting Isaac's throat. By the time that Americans first met the Loups, though, the honor of being turned to a cinder, to win a smile from the Morning Star, had been passed on to squaws captured from other nations.

As late as 1832 an American Indian agent saved a young Cheyenne woman from this fate, without, however, much prolonging her life. Although he gained custody of her, by paying an agreed ransom fee, a mob of Pawnees were in wait when he tried to ride off with the reprieved victim. Outraged by the thought of the Morning Star's disappointment, the Loups literally and without delay tore the girl to pieces.

But men and boys were also used as burnt offerings. In the course of his published *Personal Recollections*, James Ohio Pattie reported the rescue of a captured youngster by his father, Sylvester, in 1824. On this occasion the child was to have been sacrificed as the climax of a Pawnee scalp dance.

From what followed their capture, it is clear that Hugh and his friend were so luckless as to have fallen into the pyromaniac clutches of the Wolf Pawnees. For Glass, it meant an even closer call than his rub against death at Campeachy. It also meant a scar on his memory, to match the ones caused by the things he had seen and done while under Lafitte.

Pawnee religious traditions have been handed down in too incomplete a form to cover the precise ceremony of which Hugh's partner became the flaming centerpiece. The description given by Clark, though, leaves no doubt that ritual ordered the ingenuity with which human arson was here committed.

In place of being burned at the stake, as per common executions by fire, the white man was transformed into a living column of kindling by slivers of pine, each rich in resin, thrust into all regions of his bare body. Touched off, they scorched the victim's every part at once, as opposed to having destruction by fire begin at the feet and creep upwards.

In this fashion died (probably during the fall hunt of 1818 or the summer one of the following year) the one ally Hugh had found since his impressment by Lafitte.

And Glass was forced to watch this loss while clutched by the knowledge that he, too, would thus bristle with pine flares.

He had leisure to suck that wormwood. Because such murders were ritualistic, it is not likely that Hugh's black bean was promptly drawn. During the period of waiting until another suitable ceremony, moreover, Pawnee practice called for treating the victim well, out of honor to the god or spirit to which he would be dedicated.

The custom of pampering the sacrifice to be, indeed, is the one thing which accounts for the fact that Glass was not frisked even of such clothes as an Indian might covet. Hugh, therefore, had a card to play when his turn for immolation arrived, even though it didn't look to be anything but a deuce, if a trump at all.

As earlier noted, Glass had packed a few articles, to be used for trading with Indians, before he dived from the pirate ship at Campeachy. The rest he appears to have disposed of prior to being nabbed by the Wolf Pawnees, but stowed in a pocket was a package of cinnabar, the stuff to make red war paint of fireman's-hat brilliance.

Clark's wording, at this point, merely tells what Hugh did when hailed before the chief presiding at the auto-da-fé; interpretation is left up to the reader. All that can be authoritatively said, then, is that Glass was never a man to take the bludgeonings of chance lying down. He had to do something while life still allowed it, and he did it now. Moved by who knows what inspiration, or perhaps none at all but the urge of a condemned man to make some farewell gesture, in the absence of being able to say anything which would be understood, Hugh reached for his parcel of vermillion, before the sachem could roll out the order to have him incinerated. Bowing ceremoniously, next, he presented it to the astonished savage.

Immediately all was turned upside down. In a prize received from so unexpected a source the chief saw the hand of the Great Spirit signaling. Its message was that Hugh was a lucky sending, to be embraced and not destroyed. Wherefore the sagamore announced that he was adopting a man of middle years as his son, and bore him off to a feast in honor of the occasion. It is not on record that any Thanksgiving turkey has ever been whisked from under the raised ax and promoted to the status of a household pet, but if such an event ever does take place it will form the only parallel to this escape-with-honors on the part of Hugh Glass.

From then on, he was by fiat a Pawnee Loup, and he lived as one, during years in which American civilization had hardly begun to change the group's Stone Age outlook and methods of procedure. As for what he learned at this time, much was useful to him in his later career. The way of life forced upon him must have often galled a man with a bent for solitude, though.

In the field, Hugh slept in the tepee occupied by his foster father, two or three foster mothers, and a range of foster brothers and sisters. During the winter months

/ 55

his close companions were even more numerous, for anywhere from three to six families might inhabit a permanent Pawnee log-and-mud lodge.

Thirty to forty feet in diameter, these were lined with low-slung bunks. Usually curtains separated the respective space allotments of families, but privacy stood fast there. Private property, on the other hand, was respected, for each crew had its own gear; nor were meals cooked communally. These were prepared about a circular central fireplace, about a yard in diameter. The smoke, or some of it anyhow, left by a vent directly above.

At that, Glass didn't have as much to put up with as he would have had he been adopted by the Mandans. Living in North Dakota, those Indians protected their horses against the severe winters of that region by stabling them in multiple household lodges.

Yet if he'd been among the Mandans, a people living on the Missouri River, Hugh would soon have had a chance to return to the States in the company of one of the parties of French or American trappers that used the stream as a highway. As a Pawnee, and as a member of that nation's tribal group which dwelt farthest from any paths so far beaten by white men, Glass could not expect to encounter any of his own kind; and he evidently didn't.

So he lived as a savage for several years, and no doubt took the warpath as one, for the Pawnees were as regularly embroiled as any of the other large tribes of the Great Plains, their chief enemies being the Cheyennes, Comanches and Sioux. In view of Hugh's later career, on the other hand, it is worth noting that the Pawnees were on good terms with the Arikaras, a fellow nation of Caddoan stock, whose speech was so alike that of the former tribe that only the trained ear could tell one from the other.

The weapons with which Hugh went to war can be guessed as a lance and a tomahawk, as well as a gun. If firearms weren't yet common among the tribes west of the Missouri, the Arikaras lived on that trade route, and the Pawnees certainly procured some through these allies. Rifles were rarer than cheap muskets, made to swap to Indians for expensive furs; but they did turn up on the Plains. It thus may have been at this time that Glass got the firearm to which American legend has assigned a fame second only to that owned by Daniel Boone.

If Hugh did not get his fabled weapon at this time, he drew bead on man and beast along the barrel of what was known in the trade as a "fusil." And, in between shots, he acquired an education in wilderness survival which could have been gained in no other way.

For even when the hunting grounds of the West were pristine the Indians had learned, as hunting peoples have universally done, that game can range an area in boundless numbers and yet can hide from desperate human searchers by the simple process of moving to a district where the hunters are not. Wherever found, accordingly, nomad hunting tribes have had the knack of turning up emergency rations when game was scarce or missing. Having had the wisdom passed down to them, the Pawnees knew the edible properties of their region's plant, aquatic and insect life. And they knew, and taught Hugh Glass, how to get blood out of a stone, as represented by the skeleton of a buffalo.

2

.\/\.\/\.\/\.\/\.\/\.\

An Ex-Pawnee Nears a Black Cat

*The savages are greatly treacherous. We traded
with them as friends but after a great storm of rain
and thunder they came at us before light and many
were hurt.*

— LETTER BY HUGH GLASS

WHILE HUGH was winning his doctorate in wild
country philosophy, much was politically afoot
which bore upon the West. In 1819, the Federal government sought to bury the stormy question as to who
owned Texas by swapping American claims there for
outright possession of Florida. But this move so en-
raged American frontiersmen that those of Natchez fa-
thered the already-mentioned invasion of Texas, led by
James Long.

The Republic of Texas which he founded had two
points of settlement. Aside from Nacogdoches, its capital, there was the seaport of Campeachy, where the
Texas navy rode at anchor when not deployed in the
personal service of Admiral Lafitte.

A peculiarity of the fur trade up to this period had been its confinement to the Missouri River. For this alone, among all the streams of major length which cut through the Great Plains, was navigable in other than flood seasons. The Red was so clogged by masses of fallen trees that it was sometimes called "Timber River." The Canadian, the Arkansas, the Kansas and the Platte were often no more than winding sandbars, broken here and there by puddles, pools and ponds. But the Missouri was forever damp, and short of the Great Falls, in western Montana, its channel was blocked by nothing which couldn't be moved or bypassed.

So the fur traders clove to the Missouri, and where it went, they did. From their headquarters in St. Louis, they followed it past Nebraska and through both Dakotas to Montana.

Although a few strays had illegally worked the region for pelts, the era of the white trapper did not dawn in the West until 1822. Earlier, the fur trade had looked to Indians to do the trapping, while the part of the paleface was to bring trade goods up the Missouri to the markets, known as forts, there to wait for tribesmen to show up with skins to swap.

This system was a hand-me-down of tradition. On the Atlantic Seaboard, it was as old as the first French, English and Dutch colonies. It had been operative in the West for a century under French and Spanish rule.

It had been continued, following the sale of Upper Louisiana to America, through the enterprise of the United States War Department.

By setting up trading posts of its own, this Federal agency was drawing revenues from the fur trade which it was loth to share with civilians. There was another and better reason, of course. The very small United States Army had the task of policing the wild nations acquired along with the acreage of the Louisiana Purchase, and the simplest way to keep them at peace with white men was to see to it that none of the latter trespassed on Indian hunting grounds.

There were, nevertheless, a few companies which had begun doing business on the Upper Missouri before the War Department put the lid on. Thus the cry of "special privilege" could be raised by those shut out. And there were growls even from those inside, angered at finding the Federal spoon in their commercial dish.

As long as Missouri was a mere territory, its resident frontiersmen had no representatives which could command the ear of Congress. But after the Compromise of 1820 turned it into a state, the very able Thomas Hart Benton was elected as United States Senator.

Devoted to the furtherance of the West, Benton made opening the region's fur trade to free competitive enterprise one of his first projects. Young in the Senate though he was, he was so forceful that, by 1822, the War Department was obliged to grant licenses to trade in Indian territory to all applicants in good standing with the law. Yet this alone did not alter the shape of the high Missouri's commerce, for the licenses were still viewed as giving businessmen the right only to deal with Indian trappers. One man who paid the fee had a different notion, though.

William Henry Ashley, who was Missouri's first lieutenant governor, had never been up the fur trade's Rialto at this time; but he had long been pumping information out of all who had been deep in the wilderness. Among those he had interviewed were some do-it-yourself trappers, back with the beaver to buy themselves a spree. When he had compared the takes of these poachers with those of individual Indians as reported by traders, Ashley emerged with a theory which was to change the course of Western history and enliven it with a warehouse full of adventure tales.

There are, indeed, three basic chapters in the West's story, not counting the preface written by the Lewis and Clark expedition. Of these, one was the urge of American frontiersmen to take over Texas, flying whatever flag. The second was the opening of the trail to Santa Fe and allied Southwestern parts by tradesmen willing to put their scalps on the line. But the third and most far-reaching was Ashley's bid for a fortune in furs; for out of his original thinking in this connection came the straddling of the Rockies, and the trails to various parts of the Pacific Coast.

Although he had not thrown his thoughts that far west, he was still mentally ahead of everybody else in the fur trade when he was at last able to get the license which let him practice, early in 1822. Promptly he be-

gan recruiting a band of one hundred men, pledged to
an enlistment period of a couple of years. With the exception of such specialists as a blacksmith and an interpreter, these signed up as trappers. For Ashley was convinced that there was far more to be made out of furs
by sending frontiersmen in quest of them than by waiting for Indians to turn up with whatever they had seen
fit to trap between buffalo hunts, war expeditions,
horse-stealing excursions, ceremonies, councils and the
other demands of tribal life.

In partnership with Ashley at the outset was Major
Andrew Henry, who should have been awarded legendary standing — but fortune has denied him even that.
Owning Jonah's genius for bringing bad luck to others,
as well as wallowing in it himself, he was too hopeless a
case to be compared with the prophet. If the whale had
gulped in Henry, it would have then got lockjaw, forc-
ing the Major to seek another exit.

The reason Ashley teamed with this Wrong Horse
Harry was that Henry was one of the rare American
bears who had gone over the mountain, as represented
by the Rockies, and seen what there was to see.

Not that this adventure was of his own choosing. In
1810 Andrew Henry had been a member of the expedition to the Three Forks of the Missouri sponsored by the
old Missouri Fur Company, of which he was a partner.
Choosing a spot two miles above the junction of the Jefferson and Madison rivers, the traders built a post, but
that's as near as they came to doing any business. The
headwaters of the Missouri lay in Blackfoot country,

and the only trading done was in the way of missiles.

These redskins were said to have had a grudge against Americans which dated back to a skirmish with Lewis, Clark *et al*. So or not, they were the most dependable and active enemies the men of the West found among any of the tribes.

From spring to fall the fort was so besieged that none could venture afield without being attacked. Climactic was the Three Forks fight, in which around thirty whites were slain, while the disorganized rest made their getaway in two directions.

The leader of a party which fled west over the Rockies, Henry became the pioneer trader of the region by establishing a fort, on a branch of the Snake, which he named after himself. Needless to say, it housed a jinx the size of a bull dinosaur. Having moved southward, to be sure of getting clear of the Blackfeet, the Major then led his followers into Shoshonee territory. Not wanting trespassers, the Snakes took over where the Bloods and Piegans had left off.

Far from profiting in any way, those who lived through the winter at that particular Fort Henry had shaken the bony hand of starvation before they managed to make their way back east across the mountains in the spring of 1811. The first Missouri Fur Company rolled along like a tire with a slow leak for five more years. When it was flat entirely, Andrew Henry went back to St. Louis, where he mined something or other — it couldn't have been gold — until he and Ashley formed the first of several firms called "the Rocky Mountain Fur Company."

With the pertinacity common to black cats, Henry now proposed doing again the very thing which had proved disastrous a half-dozen years earlier. As though he had never heard of the Blackfeet, that is to say, he urged the feasibility of pushing up to the headwaters of the Missouri and establishing posts on both sides of the Rockies. As agreed upon, the plan embraced Ashley's notion of taking along white trappers in place of relying upon Indians to supply pelts.

Among those who answered advertisements calling for a hundred beaver hunters were several worth naming here. Daniel T. Potts was one, Jed Smith another and youthful Jim Bridger a third. It is uncertain, on the other hand, whether other related figures were with Ashley at this time, or were members of his second contingent.

Delayed by the loss of a boat, the first expedition got off to a typical Henry start. Because of it, the trappers were a long ways short of their goal when they found it expedient to build a base of operations. Located four hundred and forty yards beyond the mouth of the Yellowstone, the second Fort Henry was inside North Dakota's western border.

If the partners hadn't made as much progress as had been hoped, they now saw themselves as firmly established on the high Missouri. Thinking to use the one in hand as the anchor of a westward-stretching line of posts, Ashley left the Major in charge and returned to St. Louis, in order to find more men with whom to people the projected new stations.

So much for this pair, as of 1822, which was also a key year in the life of Hugh Glass. For word had finally reached the Pawnee Loups that it paid to come into St. Louis and make the acquaintance of the United States Superintendent of Indian Affairs. This was none other than William Clark, unchallenged as the West's first citizen since the murder of Meriwether Lewis in 1809.

Doubtless a certain Pawnee chief did get rewarded for smoking peace with the Great White Father's Missouri front man, but he lost a foster son while so engaged. Once in St. Louis, Hugh resigned as an Indian and carried on as a paleface thereafter.

He remained west of the Mississippi, too. In the absence of any words of his own on the subject, it is necessary to reason as to why he didn't return to his former haunts — in Pennsylvania, or wherever else they were to be found — when free to do so. The grounds for his failure either to seek his home or resume his career as a mariner appear plain enough, however.

It is just to suppose that a man of ripe years was married at the time of his impressment by Lafitte. What with his tour of duty as a pirate, and his later enlistment as a Pawnee, he had been absent from his presumptive home for something like five years before he reached a path which could take him back there. Tennyson had not yet written *Enoch Arden*, but it doesn't take a poet's imagination to see that a man out of ken for a lustrum might find himself replaced by a wife who had every right to think herself a widow. Hugh might have feared as much and decided not to risk what could have turned out to be a painful reunion. Or he may well have made inquiries by mail which led him to understand that he could not patch the ties which Lafitte had snapped.

Probably he did not return to the sea because of a negative reason as well as a positive one. Allergic to being hanged, say, he kept away from parts and ports where he might meet somebody who knew of his Jolly Roger days. But in all likelihood, too, he wanted to stay in the West, moved by the same attachment to wild country which was to hold so many other borderers.

What is certain is that Glass welcomed a chance to visit parts of wilderness America which he had not yet seen. Ashley's first expedition had already left St. Louis when Hugh got there in the summer or fall of 1822. But Glass was one of those whose eyes gleamed when the *Missouri Republican* of January 16, 1823, ran the following advertisement:

For the Rocky Mountains
The subscribers wish to engage One Hundred MEN, to ascend the Missouri to the Rocky Mountains,
There to be employed as Hunters. As a compensation to each man fit for such business,
$200 Per Annum,
will be given for his services, as aforesaid. For particulars, apply to J. V. GARMIER, or W. ASHLEY, at St. Louis. The expedition will set out for this place on or before the first of March next.

ASHLEY and HENRY

The Major, in the meantime, was still at the post above the Yellowstone, where sudden death for a famous man was in the making. Unlike Hugh, Mike Fink had been a legendary figure prior to faring west. With only Davy Crockett and Jim Bowie as rivals, he had become one of the folk heroes of Trans-Appalachia while yet in his lusty prime. A brute but happy about it, he had scored an unbroken string of triumphs in rough-and-tumble fights and shooting matches and in such bowers as were to be found in the bottomlands and river ports of the Ohio and the Mississippi. Professionally he had also soared, for he was reckoned the best keelboat skipper on both rivers. Writers had joined the applauders, and turned out a cycle of tales about the man who delighted to have himself referred to as "the Snag" and "the Snapping Turtle." Fink was a lucky man — until he joined the garrison of Fort Henry.

There everything went as wrong for Mike as it possibly could. His pride and joy for years had been his adopted son, a young tough known to history only as Carpenter. Devoted to Mike elsewhere, he soured on him while on the Yellowstone and gave the aging hellion the latter's first trouncing. After some months the feud was patched up by fellow trappers; but instead of improving matters, the olive branch made them worse.

To prove the return of amity, Fink and Carpenter covenanted to shoot cups filled with whiskey from each other's heads. An old game of theirs, it had given them roughhewn joy in the past; but this time the impossible happened. When Mike shot, his bullet went too low, and that was all for Carpenter.

Fink himself got drilled in the course of trying to convince a man called Talbott that he hadn't killed the thing he loved on purpose. Then, to wrap the package

up, Talbott drowned while trying to cross the Missouri
a few days later.

As there was more to come, Henry's malign medicine
was at its destructive best when Hugh Glass, cuddling
his rifle, stood by to move up the high Missouri. To do
so, he boarded either the *Yellowstone Packet* or the
Rocky Mountains, on March 7, 1823. James Clyman
was of his party. So were Tom Fitzpatrick, Bill Sublette
and Ed Rose. Whether John Fitzgerald, Hiram Allen,
Black Harris and Dutton were members of this expedition or were by then at Fort Henry are matters for
guesswork only.

But Ashley, later thought of as born with a horseshoe
in his hand, was to have no luck as long as he stayed in
harness with the Major. The 1822 junket had been
marred by the early loss of a boat. On this occasion, misfortune couldn't wait for departure before it struck.

This can be said on the authority of the *Missouri Republican* of March 12:

> Two keel boats belonging to Gen. Ashley left this place
> Monday for the Yellow Stone, for the purpose of hunting
> and trapping. . . . We understand a man fell overboard
> from one of the boats on Monday and was drowned.

Then a week later the *Republic* carried a story which
was headed AFFECTING OCCASION:

> On Thursday morning last, three men belonging to Gen.
> Ashley's expedition to the Yellow Stone were conveying a
> quantity of powder in a cart to the boats at St. Charles,
> when fire was communicated to the powder by means of
> a pipe. . . . The men were blown into the air to the
> height of several hundred feet, and the cart shivered to

pieces, and the horses much injured. One of them survived a few minutes after his descent to the ground; the others were entirely lifeless and burnt in the most shocking manner.

As another St. Louis paper estimated the strength of the party at one hundred men, four less than that now pulled away from St. Charles, bucking the strong spring current with oars abetted by sails. Yet these were not all hunters, in spite of the fact that Ashley had tried to recruit that many. Actually he was able to assemble only about half that number, for some fifty of these were described as "boatmen." Their function was to work the *Yellowstone Packet* and the *Rocky Mountains* up the river to the company's trading post, and to return from it with whatever pelts the first echelon of trappers had been able to take.

These had been divided into two parties, for in addition to the fort's garrison, fourteen men were encamped much nearer Great Falls. "I ascended the Masuri," Potts wrote, "and arrived at the mouth of the Mussel Shell, on the latter end of November where I wintered with thirteen others here was a remarkable escape of my scalp as two large parteys of Indians wintered within twenty miles of us and our better enimys the black feet . . ."

As soon as the spring thaw was far enough behind for trails to offer war parties good footing, the "better enimys" proved they hadn't softened. When the breakup of ice made it feasible, in April of 1823, Henry's advanced party moved farther up the Missouri in canoes. Potts was not long of the band, for a comrade undertook to poke into his loaded gun a ramrod which roared out and whipped through both of Daniel's knees. Two men were evidently detailed to take him back to Fort Henry, for only eleven were reported present when the Blackfeet struck.

Apparently not worrying as to whether their scalps escaped or not, this small group were west of Great Falls, near the mouth of Smith River, when a war party caught up with them on May 4. The seven still living whites hurried back to the mouth of the Yellowstone, but they hadn't seen the last of a tribe which was seldom met that far east.

Boating up the Missouri, the frontier traveler passed by turns through the territories of the related Omahas and Poncas, the Sioux, the Arikaras, the Mandans, the Hidatsas or Minitaris, the Cheyennes, the Crows, and the Assiniboins. Most westerly of all were the Blackfeet, a tribe of highlanders not properly counted as one of the nations of the Great Plains. Yet in May of 1823, the Siksikas began a series of raids upon Fort Henry, driving off mounts and pack animals in the course of each one.

Nor were Ashley's men the only ones attacked. Formed in 1819, the second Missouri Fur Company was headed by Joshua Pilcher assisted by other veterans of the trade. Not willing to be outguessed by newcomers, two of the partners had led a party into the region which Henry was trying to exploit. Moving up the Yellowstone, the men, under Robert Jones and Michael Immel, met, near Pryor's Fork, Blackfeet to the number of three to four hundred.

Neither Immel nor Jones survived to report, but one William Gordon told what took place in a letter to Pilcher:

"They lay in ambush for us on the side of a steep hill, the base of which was washed by the river, along which we had to pursue the intricate windings of a buffalo trace, among rocks, trees, etc., among which they had secreted themselves. At this place the men were, of course, much scattered for a considerable distance, as two horses could not pass abreast. At this unfortunate moment, and under circumstances so disadvantageous, they rushed upon us with the whole force, pouring down from every quarter."

The whites lost seven men. The rest, including several who were wounded, got from under only by rafting the river. While they were unhappily making their way back where they came from, the Blackfeet were joyously counting the scalps, horses and pelts they had taken.

But even before word of what had taken place on May 30 reached the mouth of the Yellowstone, Major Henry had decided that he needed more men on his side, as well as replacements for the lifted mounts. Figuring that Ashley should by then be somewhere in South Dakota, his partner asked Jed Smith to speed across country and intercept the boaters below the beginning of the Missouri's bent-bow-sweep north and west, toward Montana.

As for once the Major had guessed right, Jed found

Ashley's two keelboats a few miles below the mouth of the Grand. Flagged ashore, the General was told of Henry's pressing need for riflemen and horses.

If the news which Smith had brought was bad, the vicinity in which he delivered it couldn't have been worse. Only twelve miles up, on the west side of the stream, stood the villages of the Rees; and not counting the Blackfeet, these Indians were the only ones on the Upper Missouri who openly had their knives out for whites.

The Rees, Rickarees and Pickarees, as the Arikaras were alternately called, were comparatively advanced Indians, who not only built permanent lodges like those of the Pawnees but fortified their towns with a ditch-surrounded palisade. These defense measures were the means by which they had held their ground, after the Sioux moved from the Great Lakes region out of respect for the guns which the Chippewas had bought from the French.

A generation earlier, the Rees had been driven from strongholds in the vicinity of Pierre, but they had dug in behind improved defenses eight miles above the Grand, and the Dakotas had been unable to oust them again.

Not that they weren't aggressive themselves, when they saw a chance to strike back. A short while before Jed gave Ashley the Major's message, the river grapevine had carried news of two Arikara embroilments. Finding Sioux in the company of a Missouri Fur Company brigade led by Angus McDonald, a party of Rees had demanded their persons. Rebuffed and out-toughed on that occasion, they had lost warriors during an abortive attack on a company outpost with a lost name, located some twenty leagues downriver.

Above and beyond that feud, the Arikaras were always kittle to approach, as they sometimes undertook to fling lead at passing craft — a thing made easy by their choice of situation. For the elsewhere broad Missouri was, there, narrowed by a big sandbar, and the channel ran between it and the two linked villages.

Although Ashley was aware of all these matters, he had come to the region to get rich, at any risk to himself or those who took his hire. As things stood at the time, it seemed that the post on the Yellowstone had to be held, and horses for the men who used it for a base were another must. So, at Ashley's command, the boats proceeded toward the Arikara narrows.

Going ashore with but one equally bold companion, the General learned from the Rees that they had no feud with palefaces other than those of the Missouri Fur Company, and they were ready to call that off. What the Arikaras learned from the General was that he was very anxious for horses, which could be priced accordingly.

Still Ashley did not put his head all the way in the bear's mouth. He insisted that the trading — which began on May 31 and wasn't wound up until the next morning — should be conducted on a beach which lay between the river and the two walled villages. When the dickering was over, the General had gained forty or fifty horses, and the Indians had got what they wanted, too.

Some chroniclers have said that in his eagerness for mounts, Ashley supplied the Rees with the firearms they lacked; but according to his own report three-fourths of them already had what he described as "London fucils," the implication being that they were obtained from the Hudson's Bay Company. What they *were* short of was powder for their weapons, and this the emergency made the General willing to give them.

Meanwhile the hunters, as opposed to the boatmen, were camped on the beach. About forty in all, they were due to take the horses overland to Fort Henry, which they could reach much sooner than the keelboaters. In addition to the many extra leagues imposed on them by the river's course, these would have to cordelle their craft, or tow them while trudging along the bank, wherever the current was too strong for oarsmen to cope with.

No doubt there was fraternization, in all its variety of meanings; but by nightfall most of the forty were under canvas on the beach instead of over squaws in town. Hugh Glass was so fixed, and so were Jed Smith, Clyman, Bill Sublette, Fitzpatrick, and others whose names have been preserved in no other connection.

Ed Rose wasn't there, as he had known the Arikaras during earlier jaunts through the West — one of them a trip back from Astoria, after it was lost to the British as a forfeit of the War of 1812. He had stayed in the villages later than the rest; later even than Aaron Stephens, who had remained too long.

Having given orders for sunup starts by land and water, Ashley had gone to sleep in the belief that there was nothing to fear from the Rees after all. He first learned differently when he was waked, as he estimated, at three in the morning of June 2. Rose was on hand, and informed the General that Aaron Stephens had been killed by the Indians. Rose also said that from the way the Indians were acting, he judged that they planned a sneak attack on the men ashore.

Now, Ashley had brought some more than questionable characters up the Missouri with him in 1823. Jim Clyman, who had helped recruit them, wrote that he had combed "the grog shops and other sinks of degredation" in his search for candidates. So it was perhaps not strange that Ashley seemed untroubled by the news that Stephens had been murdered; knowing the man, he may have decided that Aaron had asked for it.

Neither was the General troubled by the news of projected Ree treachery, for the reason that he didn't believe Rose was a reliable informant on any subject. Washington Irving, who had to do with Ed in the course of his tour of the Plains, later explained why. Rose he described as "a dogged, sullen, silent fellow with a sinister aspect and more of the savage than the civilized man in his appearance."

Rose apparently owed his unpleasant outward seeming to the etchings made by his way of life on the face of a halfbreed darkened by a dash of the Congo, for Irving went on to declare: "This fellow, it appears, was one of those desperados of the frontier outlawed by their crimes, who combine the vices of civilized and savage life and are ten times more barbarous than the Indians with whom they consort. Rose formerly belonged to one of the gangs of pirates who infested the islands of the Mississippi."

So Ashley told Rose that he was ready to take on the Arikaras, and let it go at that. He was not ready for the attack that vindicated Ed, in spite of the fact that he had taken the military precaution of anchoring his two boats close inshore and bracketing the hunters' camp.

In the report in which he stated as much, the General did not, curiously, explain why the trappers were as taken by surprise as they were. It was Hugh Glass who gave the clue to that puzzle in the one piece of writing left by his hand. The men on the beach had reason to be glad of the tents they were specified as having, for there was a torrential downpour as dawn drew near.

Under cover of that watery screen, some of the Arikaras stole out of their villages and took firing positions in clumps of brush. They also manned a driftwood breastwork at one end of the sandbar. This done, they could rake the camp with fire from two directions, attack the boats from an unexpected compass point, and cut down any who might think the sandbar a refuge.

As soon as it was light enough for the Rees to see their front sights, they started burning the powder obtained from Ashley, who noted that "the Indians commenced a heavy and well-directed fire from a line extending along the picketing of one of their towns, and some broken land adjoining." The General tried to get the situation promptly in hand, but he was balked by two factors.

The first was the quality of his boatmen. Panic their master, they refused to bring the keelboats to the support of the men on land. Instead they thrashed out of firing range; and it was from there that a few sandier souls put skiffs in the water, with a view to staging a one-horse Dunkirk.

The second was the quality of his trappers. In place of wishing to flee, they were furious and tried to tough it out. So these, as Ashley wrote, refused to co-operate with their would-be rescuers: "From a predisposition on their part not to give way to the Indians as long as it was possible to do otherwise, the most of them refused to make use of the opportunity of embarking, the large skiff returned with four, two of them wounded; and was immediately started back, but unfortunately one of the oarsmen was shot down, and by some means the skiff set adrift."

By then the embattled trappers had found that shooting back at redskins covered by a palisade or concealed by brush was a nonprofit undertaking. But when they began to retreat, they discovered that the big skiff was a derelict, while "the other was taken to the opposite side of the river by two men, one mortally wounded."

After writing that, Ashley went on to describe the tragic scramble which followed: "Some swam to the boats, others were shot down in the edge of the water and immediately sunk, and others who appeared to be badly wounded sunk in attempting to swim . . ."

Of the forty who had counted on leaving for Fort Henry that morning, eleven besides Aaron Stephens were either slain outright, drowned, or had died from wounds by the time the defeated expedition had found, twenty-five miles downstream, a suitable point for encampment. Mustering his survivors, the General learned that Hugh Glass and a dozen others were wounded.

Although Ashley was for turning back and running the Ree gantlet under cover of rifle fire, he wasn't talking to listening men. The morale of the outfit had died when the boatmen had let the trappers down and the General had been unable to keep the former from fleeing. Most of both sorts were for quitting, and the thirty who volunteered to stick said they weren't going upriver again without a strong supporting force.

Pinned down by their determination, Ashley soon made his headquarters at the mouth of what he called "the Shegan," but what was doubtless the Cheyenne. But, from his first stopping point, on June 4, he wrote the quoted report to Major Benjamin O'Fallon, the United States Indian Agent at Fort Atkinson, the military post near Council Bluffs. The General wanted the army to help him take the Arikaras in hand, and he was using the proper channels.

This and other communications were taken downriver by the *Yellowstone Packet,* aboard which were the badly wounded and the many hale men who had resigned after seeing what the West was like. There weren't so many of the former as there had been, because three of the men blooded by the Rees subsequently cashed in, making the death total fifteen.

One of the thirty willing to see more of the Arikaras, Hugh Glass, also, wrote a letter which the leaving keelboat took along. Fortunately saved and ultimately turned over to the South Dakota Historical Society by a descendant of the addressee, it was unfortunately pilfered by some scoundrel of a collector — but not before it was photographed for inclusion in John G. Neihardt's *The Splendid Wayfaring*.

The top of the single sheet on which it was written was so crumbled or torn that only "Ashley's" and "June" can be certainly made out of the superscription. The text is intact, though, and so for once the man who met the bear is heard speaking with his own tongue, if one schooled to somberness by the occasion. This was the passing of a young Virginian named John S. Gardner, to whose father Hugh was writing.

DR. SIR:

My painfull duty it is to tell you of the deth of yr son wh befell at the hands of the indians 2d June in the early morning. He lived a little while after he was shot and asked me to inform you of his sad fate. We brought him to the ship where he soon died. Mr. Smith a young man of our company made a powerful prayer wh moved us all greatly and I am persuaded John died in peace. His body we buried with others near this camp and marked the grave with a log. His things we will send to you. The savages are greatly treacherous. We traded with them as friends but after a great storm of rain and thunder they came at us before light and many were hurt. I myself was hit in the leg. Master Ashley is bound to stay in these parts till the traitors are rightly punished.

Yr. Obdt. Svt.

HUGH GLASS

The young chap who made the powerful prayer was that great explorer, chronic Bible student and canny trader, Jed Smith. By the time Hugh's letter cruised off in the *Yellowstone Packet,* however, Jed was a-horseback, carrying a message to Fort Henry.

On the way east, Smith had been the bearer of a call for help from the Major. Heading west, he bore an appeal from the General.

What Ashley wanted Henry to do was to join him with every man not strictly needed to keep the Blackfeet from seizing their jointly owned trading station. Asking the Major for emergency assistance was akin to hiring Typhoid Mary as a nurse; but Ashley did it, thus bringing Hugh that much closer to his destiny.

3

⋀⋀⋀⋀⋀⋀

The Tribe That Got Away

We saved the greatest part of the flour and all the whisky . . . but we unfortunately lost fifty seven muskets and bayonets.
— REPORT BY COLONEL HENRY LEAVENWORTH

THE NEWS of Ashley's defeat at the hands of the Arikaras, and of that served the Missouri Fur Company by the Blackfeet a few days earlier, reached Fort Atkinson separately — but not much so. At the time, the post was the only one charged with policing the central and northern Plains, as well as the Rockies and whatever lay beyond. It was manned by the Sixth Regiment, a skeleton outfit which didn't have to be specified as infantry, because there was not so much as a cavalry squadron in the United States Army.

"The Colonel Commanding," as Leavenworth was given to calling himself in orders to the regiment, had established a reputation for bold and decisive leadership during the War of 1812. Additionally, he was a very pleasant fellow, who liked to forward the careers of the officers serving under him. As these in turn were proud of him, morale was high. If companies allotted one hundred men by the tables of organization only had forty-odd, they still belonged to a crack unit, with a record which hadn't known spots as the spring of 1823 ripened.

Ordered to keep the Indians in a state of savage grace, Henry Leavenworth had more or less managed it by leaving them alone. Unless they disrupted settlement, the government took the same view of intertribal wars that wise parents do of the squabbles between boys; it looked the other way and let the redskins do what came natural. Even when the Indians of the West slew an occasional white man, the War Department — which would have liked to keep all palefaces out of the region — didn't take offense. But the three reports placed on the Colonel Commanding's desk in May and June couldn't be shrugged off as unfortunate incidents:

Four Ashley men killed by the Blackfeet . . . Seven Missouri Fur Company operatives slain by the same tribe . . . The massacre in which the Arikaras took the lives of fifteen more of Ashley's trappers . . . And word came down the river that other tribes, formerly not hostile, were envious of the feats of the Blackfeet and Rees and were beginning to hanker for the scalps of white men, themselves.

In a letter which Joshua Pilcher wrote to the Fort Atkinson Indian Agent, the head of the Missouri Fur Company quoted one of his men to the following effect: "The present affair of the Ricaras is the subject of daily conversation with the Gros Ventres and Mandans; and I am of the opinion, from many remarks made by the principal men of both nations, that much of the future welfare and interest of the persons engaged in the business of the Missouri depends much upon the course pursued against that band of savage villains."

The Gros Ventres above referred to were not the allies of the Blackfeet properly so called; the traders and trappers of this period applied the name also to Hidatsas or Minitaris. The Mandans excepted, they had been better disposed toward the whites than any of the Upper Missouri Indians. So the news that these two nations were warpath-minded made grim reading. If these turned hostile, so would others, threatening an end to the fur trade.

However the War Department might feel about white exploitation of the West, there was an issue involved which Leavenworth could see, because he had been a lawyer before becoming a soldier. Had the United States bought most of the Louisiana Purchase just to let Indians range there? Some politicians took that to be the case, but the men of the frontier pressed a more searching question: Could American citizens be denied the right to enter American territory and earn a living there, if they were able to?

Although a string of Federal administrations tried to get off that hook and the problems it created, it hadn't gaffed any official stationed in the West until Henry Leavenworth felt its bite. A political as well as a military decision was involved; and he had to go it alone. His superior, General Henry Atkinson, was out of quick communications' reach, in Louisville.

To his credit, Leavenworth didn't flinch, when that news came upriver, but acted promptly and with decision. If the Missouri was to remain a commercial thoroughfare, something had to be done in the way of getting the Indians back in line, and the obvious move was to make an example of the Arikaras, as the worst offenders. On June 18 he gave orders for six companies of his regiment to prepare to go to the relief of General Ashley.

The latter, in the meantime, was still bent on seeing to it that the Rees were punished, for he had more besides the loss of his men to grind his teeth over. Hugh Glass — who was perhaps one of the wounded men salvaged by the skiff — evidently had managed to save his "favorite rifle," but most of the survivors of Arikara gunfire had left their equipment on the beach, or, as Clyman did, dropped it in the river upon finding it too heavy to swim with. Then there were the horses Ashley had bought from the Indians, and of which they had kept all that hadn't got in the way of bullets. Lastly, there was the gumboil of a thought that all this scathe and loss had resulted from gunpowder obtained from himself.

But though stewing in chagrin, the General didn't let go of his hold on reality. "The Rickarees," as he wrote, "are about six hundred warriors . . . armed with London fucils, which carry a ball with considerable accuracy and force." If totally mustered, there weren't enough whites on the Upper Missouri to hope for success, when attacking that many palisaded redskins. Unless the Army pitched in, nothing effectual could be done.

Ashley, as has been said, retained only thirty members of his second expedition. If a constant loser, Henry was ever ready to act, and upon receiving his partner's summons, the Major led fifty men away from the Yellowstone, leaving only twenty — of which one was wounded-knees Potts — to hold down the Rocky Mountain Fur Company's beleaguered post.

That added up to eighty men; the Missouri Fur Company contributed forty; a couple of dinky firms helped swell the tally, as did a scattering of border drifters. But it wasn't enough, unless the Army lent support — so the news from Fort Atkinson was welcome, indeed.

As the Sioux were enemies-in-chief to the Arikaras, Joshua Pilcher went to them. Enabled to tell the Dakotas that the braves of the Great White Father were advancing upon the Rees, Pilcher got around four hundred prompt volunteers and was promised that other bands would swell the avenging army. Of American soldiers, the redskins of the upper Missouri had seen none in action, but glib interpreters of the Indian Service had been so fulsome in telling of the government's military might that the tribesmen would not have been surprised to find a thunderbolt in the bandoleer of every rear-rank dogface. If the Arikara villages were to be blasted from the map, the Sioux wished to be in bald-headed row when that took place.

Not equipped with Thor's hammer, but taking all the weapons specified by the Colonel Commanding, two hundred and fifty members of the Sixth Regiment left

Fort Atkinson on July 22. One of their several boats was the *Yellowstone Packet,* lately chartered by William Ashley. Aboard the sundry craft were the personnel and equipment of six infantry companies, their commissary and ordnance supplies, two six-pounders and several lighter cannon, mounted on swivels.

As the troops were on their way to join forces with Major Henry, their journey could hardly have been smiled upon by the stars, and it was not. Whenever feasible the commanders of keelboats caught the wind in a two-master's canvas. But sailing in a river is tricky business — the breeze is apt to shoot from a different quarter at each new turning of the river.

If he hadn't known that before, Lieutenant William Wickliffe found it to be so on July 3. Where he got that lesson is of more interest than the date, however. Leavenworth in one of his reports said that it was in the vicinity of Cobalt Bluff, but it has since been more exactly located.

The boatmen of the Missouri had by then named every landmark which broke the monotony of jog-along, level banks. Points which soared above this mean were "bluffs"; those which dipped below it were "bottoms." And all which didn't have a distinctive appearance, as in the case of the blue clay which suggested "Cobalt," were identified with some connected event or renowned regional character.

Such a one was a chief of the Yankton Sioux called Smutty Bear, a dominant tribal figure for many years, and one who once spoke for his people in Washington.

At some point in a public career which dated back to 1815, he did something or other which caused rivermen to affix his name to a strip of water-level land near the aforesaid bluff.

Aware of this, the late Doane Robinson, of the South Dakota Historical Society, was able to make one of the most remarkable statements in the long line of scholarship. After studying the scene of Lieutenant Wickliffe's disaster, Mr. Robinson concluded that "the exact place of the accident was off Smutty Bear's bottom."

So much for the locus; now for what took place there. As has been urged before, river sailing is a hatful of surprises. Looking for more wind than he had, the Lieutenant steered into more than he wanted. It raced him toward a snag lying off the bottom in question; and he didn't try to avoid it, because, as Leavenworth explained, the upriver breeze ruffed the down-sweeping current, making the water opaque. The keelboat slammed into a stiff branch of a sunken tree, which split the craft.

Those in the other boats rallied, with a nice eye for priority. All the whiskey was saved, and most of the flour — but none of the salt pork, which the soldiers apparently didn't like. The guns and bayonets of better than half a hundred infantrymen were also casualties; and when all hands looked around, after rescuing John Barleycorn, they made another discovery. "What was still worse," Leavenworth wrote, "we found on mustering the crew that we had lost one sergeant and six men."

Five days later, wind wrecked the *Yellowstone*

Packet, though on this occasion nobody was aboard. As night had fallen, the soldiers the boat daily carried were encamped ashore. It had been believed that the craft was riding securely in the lee of a bluff, but the gale which attacked without warning, before midnight of July 8, bypassed the highland, snapped both of the *Packet's* masts, yanked the craft loose from its mooring, and drove it against a sandbar with a force which shook the deck overboard.

The philosopher who chirped that history never repeats itself didn't know the dogfaces of the Sixth Regiment. Without seeming to guess that more than coincidence was at work, Leavenworth wrote, as to this disaster, almost the same thing that he did with respect to the previous one: "We saved considerable flour and all the whiskey; and lost all the pork and also all the supplies of the officers' mess. We also had again the misfortune to lose a small number of muskets and bayonets."

But the second wrecked craft had carried cannon and ordnance stores. One of the six-pounders stayed in the river, but the other was salvaged by the regimental surgeon, Major John Gale, who appears to have known how to cope with river hazards better than any of the line officers. Gale likewise managed to fish out nearly all the cannon, all the lead for musket bullets and a barrel of powder. As Leavenworth observed, the expedition would have been forced to return to Fort Atkinson had this not remained in good condition, but when the cask was anxiously broached, it was learned that the cooper who'd made it was an honest craftsman. After hours of immersion, the powder was dry.

The condition of the *Yellowstone Packet* cheered the outfit's officers, at least. If the boat had been stove in, the regiment would have been too short of boats to make continuance possible; but the hull was sound.

So the expedition advanced toward the Missouri Fur Company post which Potts called "Cederfort," now generally referred to as "Fort Recovery." Here, or near the present town of Chamberlain, South Dakota, Leavenworth was welcomed by Pilcher, who supplied guns to replace those swallowed by the Missouri.

Here, too, the gratified Dakotas pledged their cooperation. And more joined the avengers of Ashley, until about a thousand were boating, riding and slogging afoot toward where the General himself waited with eighty trappers at the mouth of the Cheyenne.

Of these, fifty must have been brought by Andrew Henry, as the General declared that only thirty members of his second expedition chose to stay with him. Dutton may have been among those who, like Potts, had been left to man the post on the Yellowstone; but George Yount's other informant, "Allen of Mojave notoriety" was present. Jim Clyman and Moses Harris, who indiscriminately answered to the nicknames of "Black" and "Major," were there. Present, too, were Hugh Glass, John Fitzgerald and Jim Bridger.

Although Harris was said to have once held the rank of major, he didn't function as any sort of officer when Ashley marshaled his army. In offering his services to the Colonel of Regulars, the Militia General made nominations which Leavenworth approved and recorded as follows:

> Jedediah Smith for Captain
> Hiram Scott, do.
> Hiram Allen, Lieutenant
> George C. Jackson, do.
> Charles Cunningham, Ensign
> Edw. Rose, do.
> —— Fleming, Surgeon
> T. Fitzpatrick, Quarter Master
> William Sublette, Major

It is probable that the Colonel Commanding, who didn't catch Fleming's first name at all, got that of Lieutenant Jackson wrong, and that the officer in question was really the David E. Jackson later in fur-trading partnership with Jed Smith and Bill Sublette. From his position in the list, it can be judged that Bill was not a full-fledged officer but the battalion sergeant major. Lastly it can be guessed that anybody as careless about recording names as Leavenworth was probably got Allen's given one wrong. There could have been "Hirams" so paired, of course, but it's not a bet on which Lloyd's of London would risk a Confederate dollar. The chances are that the Allen known to Yount and the Reverend Orange Clark could have long ago been identified, if he had been properly named when about to advance upon the Arikaras.

The two Ree villages were on the west bank of the Missouri. The one on the lower side of Cottonwood

Creek contained seventy Pawnee-type lodges, while that above the stream held seventy-one. Trusting to their wooden walls and the shallow, dry moat which added to their height, the red burghers awaited the arrival of the motley punitive force.

The Sioux in the van, Leavenworth's army began to go into action on August 9. As the Arikaras dashed out to meet their hereditary enemies, skirmishing took place, until the first echelon of the Sixth Regiment advanced on the double. The soldiers couldn't fire, because Dakota allies stood between the infantrymen and their targets; but at sight of the Great White Father's Varangians, the Rees withdrew into their respective towns.

It developed that they were safe from attack there, a short-change of logic with but one apparent explanation. The Sioux were eager to help launch an assault. The officers and men of the Sixth wished to justify their hard journey by storming the villages. They of the Missouri Fur Company were all for it, because they believed, to use Pilcher's words, that "a decisive blow is indispensable for the safety of every white man on the river above Council Bluffs." Ashley and the men of his two expeditions were yearning to show the Arikaras that crime doesn't pay even Neolithic Man. But as Andrew Henry felt that way, too, the hope couldn't become a fact.

The clue to the failure of a far outnumbering and better-armed force to overwhelm men whose defenses were strong by primitive standards only was the strange collapse of the Colonel Commanding's spirit.

Leavenworth had dared, as few in his moccasins would have, to lead his troops against an Indian nation without the sanction of his superior officer and the War Department. His action had been as prompt as it was bold. He had been discouraged neither by two disastrous accidents nor the general hardships of an unfamiliar wilderness. And yet the man who had flown those flags, and who had a distinguished war record on file, mysteriously fell apart when he arrived where he had striven to be.

To begin with, the Sioux were a shock to the Colonel. During the War of 1812 and since, he had known Indians whose tribal ways had been modified by a certain amount of contact with civilization; but in the Dakotas of the Plains he first met Chateaubriand's unspoiled child of nature.

It has been stated above that what is known to historians as "the Arikara siege" began with vigorous action between the Rees and their ancient enemies. After the arrival of the troops had led the former to break off the engagement and retire behind their palisades, the latter indulged in a macabre romp. Cutting off the legs and arms of slain Arikaras, they dragged them about at the end of thongs, cat-calling to anguished village watchers the while. The centerpiece of the fun was provided by a Sioux draped with a grizzly's skin, who crawled from one corpse to another, growling and biting off tidbits. In recording this phase of the siege, Leavenworth morosely noted that the watching white men had been abjured not to laugh.

Whether because of that spectacle or not, the Colonel seems to have been more alarmed by his Indian allies than he was by the ones he had come to fight. The fear that the Sioux would turn on him — repeatedly expressed in his report — was surely one of the factors which favored the Rees; but at first Leavenworth went through the motions proper to an attacking commander.

Both his description and a preserved military sketch show the disposition made of his troops and supporting auxiliaries. Hugh Glass and the rest of Ashley's men were on the right flank, their line extending as far as the river. They were thus facing part of the lower village. The rest of it, and all of the upper one, were menaced by the several companies of the Sixth Regiment, marshaled in a semicircle whose northern end reached the Missouri. In reserve were the Missouri Fur Company men under Pilcher, assisted by Captain William Vanderburgh, Lieutenant William Gordon and Lieutenant Carson. Leavenworth didn't know this officer's first name; but he was Moses Carson, an older and much bigger brother of Kit's.

Angus McDonald, who had unwittingly put the Rees in the mood to attack Ashley, by trimming their feathers before he showed up, was designated as "Captain for the Indian Command." Watching with him and their other Missouri Fur Company friends, the Sioux waited for the Great White Father's supermen to blow the walls down and make the Rees accessible.

The best promise of this was the battery of cannon on a height overlooking the upper village. In the second of two not always matching reports, the Colonel Commanding said that Lieutenant M. V. Morrison was the first to make the big guns bark; but the earlier account indicates that the hot shot initially came from the hillock on the left flank, and the sketch shows that this was commanded by Vanderburgh, while that of Morrison was behind the center of the infantry line. Although a fur trader now, Vanderburgh was a former West Pointer.

But whichever directed the first cannon shot, it got the second phase of the siege off to a promising start by curing the curiosity of Chief Grey Eyes, whose head was snicked away when he peered out to see what was going on. That was not only a neat coup, but one of moment to Hugh Glass, who had known Grey Eyes while a Pawnee, and was later to meet his successor.

Yet aside from decapitating the chief and killing a mixed dozen and a half of warriors, squaws and children, the cannonading was not effective. There was seemingly no effort to use the shot to make a breach in what Ashley called "the picketing" of the villages. The big missiles (as compared with rifle bullets, that is) were lobbed amongst the lodges, which proved to be adequate shelters against that type of aerial fallout.

But the order for an assault by the infantry and the fur-trade militia never came. Not that the troops were idle the first two days. The Colonel Commanding's accounts crackled with brisk marches, clever shifts of position and daring advances down the throat of opposition. But what was actually accomplished was best told not by Leavenworth, but by H. M. Chittenden, himself a military man:

"In the operations before the Aricara villages the whites lost none in killed and but two slightly wounded. The Sioux lost two killed and seven wounded in the attack of the 9th . . . Colonel Leavenworth thought that the Aricara loss amounted to about fifty, but Pilcher was positive that it could not have exceeded thirty, including women and children, and of these thirteen had been killed by the Sioux."

In the course of actively doing nothing, the Colonel even considered plans for sapping and mining fortifications made of roughhewn cottonwood. To his great relief, however, the Rees asked for an armistice, which became effective on August 10.

"An unrestrained intercourse was immediately opened between our camp and the villages," Leavenworth reported. He added that the soldiers had visited the Indian communities with a view to purchasing "mockasins," but that can be safely doubted.

Meanwhile the chiefs, red and white, were discussing peace terms. Ashley and Pilcher wanted the Rees to return or replace the property stolen from the former, with the addition of indemnifying goods and horses. The surrender of hostages was also mooted. But the chief anxiety of the Colonel was to get back to Fort Atkinson; and when they smelled that, the Arikaras began to dictate instead of listen.

That this is what happened, Leavenworth admitted — albeit to the tune of a justifying psalm. "Considering my small force — the strange and unaccountable conduct of the Sioux and even the great probability of their joining the Aricaras against us. And also considering the importance of saving to our Country the expense and trouble of a long Indian warfare . . . I thought proper to accept the terms."

In so doing, incidentally, he stepped out of his allowed bounds. Treaties with tribes were supposed to have been drawn up by representatives of the Office of Indian Affairs, and there were two such present, in the persons of Major Henry and Joshua Pilcher. Only part-time Indian agents, both refused to function at all upon learning what the Colonel was willing to concede. So Leavenworth himself drew up the treaty which testified that the murderers of fifteen whites were only asked to give back the confiscated equipment of the dead men, plus some buffalo robes, to pay for the mounts Ashley had bought and lost. The Rees professed to be unable to forfeit horses, laying their shortage of stock to the Sioux.

Chittenden stopped short of calling the Colonel pusillanimous, but not very far:

"The conduct of Colonel Leavenworth was so vacillating and ineffectual, and apparently governed by such an undue estimate of the obstacles in his way, and such a dread of incurring any loss, that he disgusted the Indian allies, forfeited their friendship and cooperation, and excited the contempt and amazement of the trappers. . . . There is no reason to suppose that an assault on the towns would not have been successful, and from every point of view it was imperative upon Colonel Leavenworth to attempt it. Why had he come this great distance, if it was not to inflict summary punishment upon these people? Instead of doing so he fairly begged them for peace . . . and completed a treaty which he was compelled to write himself because the duly constituted officers of the government flatly refused to participate. . . ."

The Colonel Commanding didn't have his way without argument. If all the traders and trappers were disappointed by Leavenworth's chosen course, Joshua Pilcher didn't hide the fact that he was furious. His were not the men who had been slain and robbed by the Rees; but, as a veteran of the Upper Missouri, he clearly saw what a policy of appeasement would wreak in the future.

The peace talks of August 11 and 12, indeed, turned up the liveliest action of the siege, not counting the Sioux onslaught on the first day. Of an interpreter named Colin Campbell, Leavenworth noted that he "continually kept his thumb on the cock of his rifle. He also snatched a pipe tomahawk from one of the Indians and threw it to the rear."

Although disappointed in the turn of events, themselves, the Colonel's regular officers did not take part in any hostile demonstrations during the parleys. The surgeon, Major Gale, was more militant, though.

Told by Pilcher that the Indians might try for even better luck by seizing Leavenworth and holding him for ransom, Gale went into action. "The Doctor," his commander wrote, "accordingly fired his pistol at them [the

Arikaras], and Mr. Pilcher ordered Campbell to fire, he did fire, as did also Mr. Vanderburgh." Responding in kind, the Rees nicked Pilcher, but that was the only damage done. The exchange of shots caused a recess in the peace talks, however, for as the Colonel tersely put it, "We parted in a hurry."

Aware of the split in white thinking and the dominant role of the appeaser, the Arikaras next welched on the terms of the easy treaty. After bringing Ashley three rifles, one horse and sixteen buffalo robes, they said they were unable to do more.

They were not the only Indians in the vicinity who felt that the myth of the Great White Father's military might had been exploded, leaving them free to act accordingly. Without bothering to mention their plans, the Sioux decamped, and to further show their contempt, they took along a half-dozen army mules and as many again of Ashley's horses.

Meanwhile the failure of the Rees to take more than token notice of their treaty obligations had stoked Pilcher's wrath anew. Knowing this, and afraid that the Missouri Fur Company prexy might yet have his way, the Arikaras packed up during starlit hours which the whites were devoting to wrangling.

How several thousand people possessed of horses and dogs could have left the neighborhood of a military camp without being detected is not easily imagined; but Leavenworth wrote that this remarkable disappearing act took place: "Early on the morning of the 13th, we found the Ricaras had left their towns during the night."

The troops tried to round the runaways up, but the Indians had too much of a start. Upset by this development, the Colonel commissioned an interpreter named Toussaint Charbonnau (husband of Sacagawea, the semimythical girl guide of the Lewis and Clark expedition), to ride after the Rees, taking with him a peace pipe, an American flag and a related message:

"These will convince you that my heart is not bad. Your villages are in my possession; come back and take them in peace, and you will find everything as you left them. If you do not come back, there are some bad men, and some bad Indians, who will burn your villages."

As the "bad Indians" were presumably the Sioux, these were no longer present. But the "bad men" — undoubtedly Pilcher and other Missouri Fur Company operatives — were still lurking in the vicinity of the deserted villages, as Charbonnau galloped off on August 14.

When the interpreter didn't get results, the Colonel Commanding decided to call the Arikara campaign a closed one. Yet he didn't quite forsake the Rees, for he left a charge of quarters. The one selected was, though, debatably able to cope with the suspected schemers of arson.

"On the morning of the 15th," Leavenworth reported, "we placed the mother of the late Chief, 'Grey eyes' (an aged and infirm woman, whom they had left in their flight) in one of the principal lodges of the lower village, gave her plenty of provisions and water, and left her in quiet possession of the towns and the property left by the Indians."

The female parent of Grey Eyes proved unequal to the near occasion. While the villages were still within sight of the departing soldiers, Angus McDonald and William Gordon set them afire.

This act, which was wrought by fierce scorners of Leavenworth's jellyfishing, was the only one which justified the summarizing boast which the Colonel made: "The blood of our countrymen have been honorably avenged, the Ricaras humbled, and in such a manner as will teach them, and other Indian tribes, to respect the American name and character."

Chittenden took another recorded view of the siege's outcome: "The whole conduct of the fight, if such it can be called, had only served to detract from the credit of the national arms."

As that was the feeling of all but Leavenworth, the Rees' escape from chastisement was scored as an Indian victory. Something more must be said of the campaign. If indecisive and even comic when viewed from certain angles, the episode was one whose result bore hard, time and again, on Hugh's career to come.

Had the Sixth Regiment attained its supposed goal of awing the nations of the Plains in 1823, the chances are that many later battles between the army and various Western tribes would not have taken place. So much for negative guesswork. But it can be positively said that the outcome of the Arikara siege shifted the gears of the West's destiny by making Ashley discard old thinking with respect to the Missouri River.

That great stream, as above posted, had been held the fore-and-aft of the fur trade. Henry still thought it was, and he voiced a determination to push on up to the Missouri's headwaters, as originally planned.

As this had not been achieved under more favorable auspices, far less was to be hoped of the scheme now. While the region's tribes could be foreseen as more hostile, the partners had a much smaller following than had been theirs the year before. Although they had counted on adding to the men recruited in 1822, the abortive siege had turned up contrary toes. Fearful of the consequences of the mishandled Arikara campaign, many members of both of Ashley's expeditions had decided to go back to the States.

After leaving the Ree villages, the trappers dogged the soldiery as far as the Grand, and there Ashley and Henry held a final conference. On the following morning the General fared on south, while the Major headed west.

During the ensuing month, the General was to make his paying gamble to revive the sick fur trade by forgetting about its Indian-blocked aorta and sending men overland in quest of a pass through the Rockies which the Blackfeet didn't guard. It does not appear, however, that he had let this cat out of his mental bag as early as mid-August. Yet he must have known more or less what he was going to do, or he wouldn't have subtracted a dozen from the number of men whom Andrew Henry meant to lead or send to the Yellowstone. Included in those who followed Ashley downriver, on the morning of August 16, were Jed Smith, Jim Clyman, Tom Fitzpatrick, Bill Sublette and Ed Rose. As evidenced by the fact that he had been made an ensign for the Arikara campaign, Rose was more favored by Ashley after he had proved a true prophet with respect to Ree treachery.

As for the men left with Major Henry, Potts wrote that they totaled thirty. But of these, seventeen must have been assigned to the task of working the supply-laden *Rocky Mountains* up the Missouri. The Major in personal command, the residue halved the mileage of the big river's roundabout course by moving toward the fort by the Yellowstone, via the valley of the Grand.

According to Clyman, there were thirteen in the party, of which eight can be identified. Major Henry was one, Hugh Glass a second, John Fitzgerald a third and Jim Bridger a fourth. Whether or not his first name was Hiram, Yount's friend Allen was along. On the basis of statements which he himself made, it can be affirmed that Black Harris was of the group. Because of the fates which overtook them, the names of Auguste Neill and James Anderson were bequeathed to history.

Owing to loss of mounts to the Arikaras and the Sioux, his party was not equipped to make the haste Henry desired. There were only enough horses to serve as pack animals. Leading these afoot, through brush and tall grass, the trappers were slowed to less than a good walking pace. If they made twenty miles a day they were doing well.

Although Edmund Flagg's informant told him that "the Chian" was the river they were following, logic as well as other testimony bear out James Hall's statement that "their route lay up the Grand River." While the Cheyenne would take followers southward and away from the mouth of the Yellowstone, the headwaters of the Grand are in North Dakota and near those of the Little Missouri, whose valley at one point is less than thirty miles from the river near which Fort Henry stood.

The usual luck of the man that fort was named for was not long in asserting itself. According to the *Missouri Intelligencer*, which subsequently drew upon the recollection of Black Harris, this took place four days after the August 16 starting date:

About the 20th of August, Major Henry's party, on their way to the mouth of the Yellow Stone, and at a considerable distance from the Missouri, were discovered and fired upon by a war party of Indians. Two men were killed named James Anderson and Auguste Neill — two others were wounded and two horses lost.

Some chroniclers have said that the raiders were Rees, but that is contradicted by Potts and Harris, eminent authorities both. The latter declared that upon visiting one of the Mandan villages the next year, he recognized one of the horses which had been lifted along the Grand. The former wrote, in his letter of July 7, 1824, that Henry and those with him "where fired on by the Mandans and Groosvants in the dead hour of the night and killed two and wounded two more of our men two guns where fired from our men and killed one Indian and they retreated."

As has been earlier explained, the "Groosvants" were not the Gros Ventre Indians lumped with the Blackfeet because of their alliance with that ever-hostile tribe. These Gros Ventres were the normally friendly Hidatsas. The presence of the Mandans is likewise noteworthy. Only once in their history did these tribesmen ever turn upon American whites, and it was a party led by Andrew Henry that they assailed.

A couple of months earlier Pilcher had warned O'Fallon, the Fort Atkinson Indian agent, that the Mandans and Minitaris had become dangerously excited by the news of the massacre of whites by the Arikaras. Running across Henry's crew, while perhaps out looking for Dakotas, they had shown that the Missouri Fur Company's chief knew what he was talking about.

It was a short-lived war. Black Harris was later told by Mandans that the ones who had made the attack had not yet heard of the burning of the Arikara villages. The news of that conflagration cooled off savages who reasoned that their own towns might be next on the arson list, and they straightway buried the hatchet.

But that nearing reform movement was no comfort to the white men digging two graves beside the Grand. If the fight took place in the dark, the signs unveiled by sunrise would have told veterans like Henry who the raiders were; and the truth wasn't cheering. For when Indians who had always been friendly took to shooting at whites, what was to be expected of the forever war-minded Sioux?

Every day brought a chance of finding out, for as advertised by the modern name of the region, they were in Dakota territory. So, for all they knew, were the vengeful Rees, that tribe of displaced wanderers. Then, too, Cheyenne allies of the Sioux and Pawnee enemies might at any time be encountered.

Hardy frontiersmen though they were, it was a nervous group of trappers that strode on west, after putting earth above their dead. Except for Hugh Glass, that is, and possibly Black Harris. By most accounts the first, and according to one report the other, too, were as nonchalant as though they had never heard that Indians had scalping knives.

PART II

The Man Who Met a Bear

4

∧∧∧∧∧∧

He Wouldn't Oblige by Dying

Here a conversation was holden, and it was resolved that Glass should be left with two of his companions, Fitzgerald and Bridges.

— EDMUND FLAGG

O NE OF THE difficulties confronting Westerners anxious to pass through Indian country unobserved was that they lived largely on fresh meat, provided by animals which wouldn't do so until shot. The risk of being heard by redskins had to be run, for they had practically nothing else to eat; and in summertime the cutlets of any kill were very soon out of fashion. Flesh with the juices of life still in it was, moreover, the one thing which made their narrow diet tolerable to the system. From meat still flushcd with blood, the human stomach could draw the properties of vegetable nourishment, and even of the salt that wilderness rangers had learned to do without.

So Henry had to allow shooting, but he sought to reduce it to the minimum by commissioning two pot fillers, who alone were supposed to fire at anything but Indians. In James Hall's account, Glass was named as one of the pair sent ahead of the main party to scout for game; but for all his experience with the Pawnees, Hugh was a newcomer to the Upper Missouri country, whose old hands probably thought of him as a tenderfoot. Yount was undoubtedly right in saying that Henry picked two others.

Of these one was called Allen and was described by Clark as "a bosom friend of Yount's." Probably he was identical with the owner of that surname whom Ashley had nominated as an officer for the Arikara campaign. Feeling that Allen was one of his ablest hands, Henry counted on him to hunt for the crowd and watch for Indians while doing so. If Yount told Clark the name of the man sent with him, it didn't get into the record.

The rest were supposed to cluster behind Henry, but according to Flagg's version there were two self-appointed exceptions. After naming Major Henry as the commander, Flagg wrote:

"The expedition was a small one, and, as the roving tribes of the vicinity were by no means friendly, strict orders were issued that the party should move on compactly and in order and that none of the hunters should on any account separate from the main body. But the commands of the leader of an expedition to the Rocky Mountains are not observed with quite the punctiliousness of a military corps, and accordingly, notwithstanding the strict injunction to the contrary, two men, one of them named Hugh Glass and the other George Harris, strolled off from the company unnoticed in search

of wild fruit, which in that region in this season is said
to be most delicious."

Flagg's informant rechristened Moses Harris and
made him George, but that in itself doesn't give his
story the lie. In letters written three days apart, for instance, Ashley gave different first names to several
men of his who had been killed by the Arikaras. To give
one example, he called the chap, in whose behalf Glass
wrote a letter of condolence, Joseph as well as John.

So Black Harris may have joined Hugh, or he could
have been one of the two men who did so in Philip St.
George Cooke's account. Yount and Clyman, however,
imply that Glass was the only one who refused to blend
with the group; and both of them unquestionably got
their data from men who'd been present, and annoyed
by a truancy which mocked standard procedure. Acting
for Yount, besides, Orange Clark made it plain that
Hugh habitually chose his own company, and a fico for
all who didn't like his practice: "Glass as was usual,
could not be kept in obedience to orders with the rest
but persevered to thread his way alone through the
brush and chapparal. As the two [appointed] hunters
were wending their way up the River, Allen discovered
Glass dodging along in the forest alone" — and told his
companion that he hoped Hugh would get his comeup-
pance by stumbling across such a monster as he did
indeed soon meet.

When that happened is the next question. The only
one to touch on this point, Cooke stated that Hugh's

greatest adventure began "near night" on the fifth day. This again would be August 20, the day capped by a midnight Indian raid, according to the estimate of Black Harris. The date was probably farther up the calendar than that, though: Hall fixed the site as one that was three hundred and fifty river miles away from Fort Kiowa, which would mean that the Missouri had been left fifty leagues to the rear; and pedestrians living off the country, as well as leading horses, couldn't cover that much ground in just five days.

As Yount and Clyman didn't speak up here, there are only the accounts of Cooke, Flagg and Hall to rely on. The versions of the first two of these three glitter with geographical impossibilities. However vague as to other matters, Hall's narrative shows him to have been well informed as to the layout of the region, so he seems entitled to credence.

All factors weighed, it would be logical to hazard that on about August 23 Henry's party was not far from the town of Grand River, South Dakota. In that vicinity of place and time, Hugh Glass shrugged off orders and picked his own path through country he wished to inspect with no one in his hair.

The man who did this had been shaped by forces which made it natural for him to be at once indifferent to the opinions of others and careless of his own skin. He had had what might be called four incarnations, so separate from one another were the various epochs of his career. There had been the pre-Western existence, of which he never spoke beyond saying that he had been "a mariner." On the doorstep of middle age, he had been pared away from all the associations he had owned as a decent seafaring man, and had wallowed in slime beneath the scull and crossbones. Escaped from corruption, he had been dragged back to the Neolithic era by the Wolf Pawnees. Now, he had climbed halfway back up the centuries, roving with other homeless, white hunters.

The man who had survived to make that comeback was bound to have grown calluses where once he had had nerves, and Yount said as much through Clark. Hugh they jointly described as "bold, daring, reckless and eccentric to a high degree; but was nevertheless a man of great talents and intellectual as well as bodily power. But his bravery was conspicuous beyond all his other qualities for the perilous life he led."

Yet he was the one to whom a dying young man had entrusted the task of family notification, which Hugh had faithfully performed. Elsewhere in the Clark manuscript, furthermore, Glass is cited for nobility: "He had his failings. But his fellow trappers bear testimony to his honor, integrity and fidelity. He could be relied on — and no man would fly more swiftly, nor contribute more freely to the relief of a suffering fellow man than he."

Sunk amidst depravity, Hugh had surfaced undepraved. Living as a savage, he had become no part of one. It was a man with a skinful of character that strode toward his meeting with Old Ephraim.

The hunters of the West called grizzlies of both sexes that, though their everyday term was "white bear." If this was descriptive of an appearance which generated the later nickname "silvertip," the other described its disposition. For whoever first called a grizzly bear after a Biblical figure had in mind the payoff injunction of a phrase dealing with the character referred to: "Ephraim is wedded to his idols; *leave him alone*."

There were reasons why the grizzly should have expected to be allowed to follow his own bents, undisturbed by any opposers. Even when not provoked, the great bruins of that era were apt to attack men instead of avoiding them, as their descendants learned to do. Averaging nine feet of length and a half a ton as to weight, they had been cocks of America's Western walks while the Stone Age prevailed. In the eyes of Indians, slaying a white bear was a greater feat of war than killing a rival brave, and many a frontiersman came to sympathize with that point of view before the advent of the repeating rifle tipped the odds against silvertips and their cinnamon-colored variants.

A rider could deal with Old Ephraim confidently, as a horse could outrun him, where a grounded human being could not. Yet a cavalier had better not get too close, as Jed Smith once found out — and perhaps voiced as powerful a prayer as he did at the funeral of John Gardner. For a grizzly grabbed Jed's horse by the tail and was dragged fifty yards or so, before tiring of the game.

So Smith got away unscathed. But Hugh Glass was afoot as he neared a thicket in which a giantess among white bears was resting in the company of her young.

Flagg and Yount not participating, what then took

place is described in several ways. Hall wrote that the beast was so near, when Hugh was first aware of it, that it charged and caught him ". . . before he could set his triggers . . . he was seized by the throat, and raised from the ground.

"Casting him again upon the earth, his grim adversary tore out a mouthful of the cannibal food which had excited her appetite and retired to submit the sample to her yearling cubs, which were near at hand. The sufferer now made an effort to escape, but the bear immediately returned . . . and seized him again at the shoulder; she also lacerated his left arm very much, and inflicted a severe wound on the back of his head. . . ."

Veteran frontiersmen, though, have pointed out that it was impossible for a hunter to be utterly surprised by a grizzly. They have insisted that a man could *always* get off a shot, because of the monster's method of fighting. The primary war tools of Old Ephraim were not his teeth but his terribly armed forepaws. In order to be able to swing with these, he broke his charge and rose up on his hind legs, giving ample time in which to launch an aimed bullet.

Supported as he is by Clyman, as well as the mountain-man tradition picked up separately by Ruxton and Sage, Cooke is doubtless correct in showing that the only thing which saved Hugh's life was the shot he was able to fire. But though ultimately taking effect, it didn't settle for the bear until after the animal had nearly done for Hugh.

When bringing Hugh and Old Ephraim together, Cooke shows something of Cooper's talent for philosophizing while the reader waits for crucial action to begin:

"A contest with a white bear, more tenacious of life than a buffalo, is always dangerous; to insure a probability of success and safety, all the energies must arise in proportion to the magnitude of the danger, and they must be shown in perfect coolness; the slightest falter, which with the many would result from a loss of this presence of mind, would render the case hopeless and assure destruction.

"Glass would gladly have retreated, but he knew all attempts would be useless. This desperate situation only nerved *him* to the combat. All depended on the success of his first and only shot; — with an aim, cool and deliberate, but quiet, lest greater rapidity in the animal should render it more uncertain, he fired his rifle. The shot was a good one, eventually, mortal, but its immediate effect was only to raise to its utmost degree the ferocity of the animal, already greatly excited by the sight and opposition of its intended prey; it bounded forward with a rapidity which could not be eluded, in pursuit of its flying adversary, whom danger, with means of defense, had inspired with deliberate action, but now only gave wings for his flight."

Unlike Hall, Cooke knew how a grizzly fought. Caught in spite of his wings, Hugh "was crushed to the earth and rendered insensible to all but thoughts of instant death. The act of contact had been two blows, inflicting ghastly wounds, the claws literally baring of flesh the bones of the shoulder and thigh."

In contrast to the detailed accounts of Hall and Cooke, Clyman's description is a model of tabloid reporting. Of Andrew Henry's party, James wrote:

"Here a small company of I think (13) men were furnished a few horses onley enough to pack their baggage they going back to the mouth of the Yellow Stone . . . on the way they were actacted in the night. . . Mr. Hugh Glass who could not be rstrand and kept under Subordination he went off the line of march one afternoon and met with a large grissly Bear which he shot and wounded."

Clyman knew about Old Ephraim at first hand, having once sewed back on Jed Smith the ear lost in the course of such a meeting. In presenting the silvertip's reaction to Hugh's bullet, he wrote, "the bear as usual attacted Glass he attempted to climb a tree but the bear caught him and hauled him to the ground tearing and lacerating the body in a fearful rate."

Floating tradition said that Hugh fought the beast at close quarters, when cornered; and as many lesser Western figures were known to have done likewise, it can be well believed that Glass didn't give up until he had to. If he may not have owned the pistol or two cited by Sage and Ruxton, he can be seen as stabbing and slashing with the knife which he was also said to have wielded.

Not for very long, though. Raked alow and aloft by

three-inch talons, and mangled by teeth as terrible, he could soon do nothing but scream for help.

There are different reports as to how effective this was when it came. In telling of the bear's repeated assaults, Hall wrote that "In this second attack the cubs were prevented from participating by one of the party who had rushed forward to the relief of his comrade. One of the cubs, however, forced the newcomer to retreat into the river, where, standing to the middle in water, he gave his foe a mortal shot, or to use his own language — 'I burst the varment.' "

While writing to much the same effect, Flagg named the decoy and gave him a better reason for running than the one handed to the anonymous fugitive in Hall's narrative. After first remarking that the main body of Henry's party had heard Hugh's anguished yells, Flagg went on as follows:

"The first and most natural impression of the hunters was, that a band of hostile Indians were about to make an attack on them. . . . But no savages appearing and the shrieks for help still continuing and with increased vehemence, the party were making preparations for recrossing the Chian, when Harris suddenly rushed out of the woods on the opposite side and plunged into the water — a grizly bear pursuing close in his rear. Perceiving help at hand, he turned and discharged his rifle at the monster [which in this account turned out to be the mother bear and not a cub]."

Cooke, as mentioned above, had given Hugh a pair of companions. Agreeing that the parent grizzly had been drawn off, he has this to say of the action following the dreadful wounds inflicted upon Glass:

"Not sated with this work of an instant, the bear continued to pursue, with unabated speed, the flight of the two hunters . . . the fear of a horrid death, the excitement of exertion — together producing a velocity seldom equalled by bipeds."

Such a chase must have been staged, though involving the lone man of Hall and Flagg rather than Cooke's pair. Allen told Yount that he and his fellow were the first to examine Glass, but that doesn't preclude a previous try at intervention on the part of a hunter who was given grounds for heading elsewhere. This may have been Black Harris, and the episode could help explain why he didn't speak of Glass when mentioning other disasters of Andrew Henry and his unmerry men.

But it seems certain that the bear shot by Harris, or whoever the man was who it brought to bay in the river, was one of the yearling grizzlies. For accounts, which include that of Cooke, show that after her typhoon of fury let her down the parent bear found herself too injured by Hugh's bullet to follow any enemy very far.

Cooke, indeed, draws a clear sketch of a dying animal's loss of purpose. For after describing the frenzied speed of fleeing men, and the even better effort born of the beast's rage, "Borderer" continued: "But, fortunately, it could not last; — it was expended in the distance, from loss of blood; — its exertions became more feeble; — the sacrifice of a deserted comrade had saved their lives; — they reached the camp in safety."

The grown silvertip of this account was next sought and finished by a group of hunters. Where this took place, Cooke didn't state, but other versions agree that the bear died near Glass, while in most it breathed its last squarely on top of him.

So "the large grissly Bear" had had its day, and all who looked Hugh over thought that he had come to the end of his share of time, too. According to Flagg, Glass had "not less than fifteen wounds, any one of which under ordinary circumstances would have been considered mortal." Yount told Clark that one of these was a tear in the throat which spurted a red bubble every time Hugh breathed. Then there were lacerations of his scalp, his face, his chest, his back, one shoulder, arm, hand and thigh. These were specifically mentioned, and the bear may have ripped and chewed other parts of his body as well. The summarizing statement of Potts can therefore hardly be quarreled with. Hugh Glass had been "tore nearly all to peases," and the wonder is that he kept enough blood inside him to hold life there.

But to the dismay of the men who rolled the dead bear off what they thought was a dead hunter, the shocking human wreck which came to view throbbed with a pulse and stirred in time to the ebb and flow of breath. They waited, but as Glass still didn't die, they did the little enough that they could for him.

They had no medical supplies. First aid on the Plains consisted of bracing a man with brandy and tying him up with strips of a probably not laundered shirt. Because of his ripped throat, Hugh could doubtfully take the brandy, but, to use Flagg's words, "his wounds were bound up, though it was thought by all, that he could not possibly survive."

As Clyman said that the meeting with Old Ephraim took place in the afternoon, Cooke's "near night" is perhaps correct. In any case they camped in the vicinity, sure that dawn would show them nothing more difficult to deal with than another corpse to bury.

But Hugh was still unfit for a grave when the sun came up again. Although he continued to look as though he'd slip out the final exit at any moment, each gasp for breath was trailed by another.

It was a hard happening for decent men, whose lives he was endangering by hanging on to his own. As Hall put it, "The safety of the whole party — being now in the country of hostile Indians — depended on the celerity of their movements."

Nevertheless, as Allen told Yount, they first chose a solution to their problem which greatly slowed their progress. Although most of the other narrators didn't know of this development, Flagg concurred: "A litter was constructed from the boughs of trees, and during that day and the succeeding one he was borne onwards, as a corpse upon a bier."

Where they didn't have deep grass to contend with, the men who shouldered this burden had to pick their way through what Hall described as "thickets of brushwood, dwarf-plum trees, and other shrubs, indigenous to a sandy soil." In his manuscript, Clark pointed out that the nature of the load made their task doubly painful for the bearers, to say nothing of the man who quaked with new agony at every step of their uneven forward trudging.

Andrew Henry, meanwhile, was worried about the men he'd left where Blackfeet ranged, as well as the menaced party under his immediate command. But even the jogging, which brought his unclosed wounds no good, didn't keep Hugh's heart from working with the bottom dollar of blood left him by the bear. So the Major fretted while the men he wanted to speed to the fort on the Yellowstone walked at the pace of the pallbearers they resembled. And from time to time they stopped, either to shift the litter from one set of carriers to another, or to give Glass a respite from the torture they knew they were inflicting.

It is uncertain how long they proceeded in this fashion. Yount thought it was endured by all concerned for several days, possibly as many as six. Flagg's informant told him that it was two and a bit. "On the third day," according to this version, "the party arrived at a fine grove . . . in the middle of which was a large spring, supplying a creek."

Looking this spot over, Henry decided that it was a good one in which to stop risking all his men on behalf of one he had long considered as bad as gone. But as he could not bring himself to order the outright desertion of an invalid, he offered a proposition to any two takers. While he wouldn't order anybody to mark time in a danger zone, he promised to reward the pair who'd volunteer to put the pennies on Hugh's eyes, leaving the rest free to hurry on.

The accounts do not agree as to the sum of money which the Major asked men to weigh against their lives, and Hall was not specific. "Major Henry," he wrote, "by offering an extravagant reward, induced two of his party to remain with the wounded man until he should expire. . . ." Cooke declared that the amount was eighty dollars, which scarcely seems dazzling, but which may have tempted men who had snapped at Ashley's offer of two hundred dollars per annum. Other opinions weigh in at three hundred and four hundred pieces of eight bits, respectively; and looked at over the period's pay scale, these sums might be viewed as "extravagant." Why not? If a man made a quick grab for a bundle of cash equal to his normal earnings of many months, he was betting his scalp against nothing paltry.

Still, there was no subway rush of takers. The two who agreed to stay with Hugh didn't have to fight for the chance — a thing to be plunked in their favor. If they came to regret their decision, they were gritty to make it; and the sigh of relief breathed by the men who didn't speak up, but heard them do so, can all but be heard today.

Hall did not name either of the two gamblers. Yount and Cooke both said that one was a man called Fitzgerald, while the other was an unnamed youngster of seventeen. Only Flagg, of the older chroniclers, identified Fitzgerald's partner, though he caught the name as "Bridges." Subsequently, Chittenden learned from Joseph La Barge what insiders had long known: the companion of the little-noticed John Fitzgerald had gone on to become the justly celebrated Jim Bridger.

Fitzgerald and a youth of seventeen . . . Born in Virginia in 1804, Jim had turned nineteen by August of 1823; but the age assigned him by Cooke and Yount points to him, too. Insofar as is known, he was the only member of either of Ashley's first two expeditions who wasn't at least twenty-one. He was the "kid" of the outfit then — and one of the great men of the mountains later. Perhaps his age, when reaching for Henry's offer of money, was deliberately lowered by well-wishers who wanted to stress the fact that Jim's error was a youthful mistake which shouldn't figure on his score card as an adult. But assuredly there were men that could have told, who made it their practice not to. Clyman knew. His knowledge is doubtless what kept him from telling what happened, after Hugh was mangled by the grizzly; for Bridger was a friend of the other James. Yount, as well as Cooke's anonymous informant, also knew what even La Barge didn't divulge while Bridger was still alive. Yet they mumbled something about a fellow called Fitzgerald and a seventeen-year-old boy.

Fitzgerald was freely named for precisely the two reasons that Bridger was not. He did not build a later reputation which admirers were loth to smudge, and he had done what he did when of an age to be fully responsible.

Whether either of the two had been close to Glass, or had struck up a partnership between themselves, are questions with one doubtful answer. In his *Song of Hugh Glass* John Neihardt wrote that Jim — whom he calls "Jamie" and doesn't supply with a last name — volunteered because he was a protégé of Hugh, who had undertaken to school the youngster in wilderness lore. But it would be impossible to decide (and impertinent to ask) if that is an invention of the poet, or one of the floating traditions he said that he garnered while in the West during his spring days.

There is nothing else to suggest that either Fitzgerald or Bridger had any but the motives of bold mercenaries, when they took a chance on living to spend the waved dollars. Nor is there a hint that they acted other than individually.

But if they weren't close friends before, they must have edged together when they saw the remaining eight men lead the packhorses away. The whole party had been nervous while striving to speed through the region as a band. Now there were only two, pledged to the far harder course of making no moves to dodge danger. It was around them like smog — smelled and felt but not seen; and they had no ally but a man thought to be dying.

Hugh, as the hours played slow-motion follow-the-leader, showed no more disposition to get better than he did to pass on. From time to time his gashed throat worked, as it took a little administered water. Otherwise he lay still on the pallet which had been rigged for him, swathed in bandages which resembled a red winding-sheet. He could not speak; in fact his breathing seemed too feeble to draw a note from his vocal chords.

Fitzgerald and Bridger, as Flagg observed, were rooks waiting for a corpse, and not nurses:

"This [Henry's] arrangement was undoubtedly, under the circumstances of the case, the most merciful and considerate which could have been adopted. But what a situation! A man languishing under fifteen frightful wounds thousands of miles from all surgical succour — surrounded by roving savages — almost destitute of the necessaries of existence, and in the care of two lawless men whose interest it was that their patient should, as soon as possible, cease to live."

While awaiting the release for which they, of course, wished, the pair had two main occupations. They could watch for nearing war parties— Arikara, Mandan, Minitari, Cheyenne, Pawnee or Sioux — or they could feel a pulse whose languor raised their hopes, before a feeble beat let them know that they couldn't seek safety yet.

They held out against the pressure for a number of days: four, according to Yount, though Hall said five and Flagg went as high as six. Inevitably they must have grown more like buzzards, though without having that bird's genial feelings toward the dead. They must, in fact, have come to regard Hugh as an arrant enemy rather than a friend in bad straits. Every time he breathed again, he gave Indians time to ride that much nearer; and from that awareness to the suspicion that Glass was conspiring for their downfall would be no great jump of illusion for a couple inching toward a nervous breakdown apiece.

It was the man and not the boy who cracked first. If speechless, Glass could hear, and he told Yount as much, together with some of the arguments Fitzgerald used in urging Bridger to cave, too.

His points stemmed from logic, even though hysteria voiced them. First, naturally, he declared that sacrificing their own livcs would not float that of a man whom they both knew to be halfway down the deep six. The rider was that they had already earned their money by staying with Hugh much longer than Major Henry had had any notion they would be called upon to do.

This can be seen as true. It can be gathered from Yount's report that Glass had developed a fever intermittent with attacks which had the appearance of what used to be called "death sweats." It was doubtless one of these which had pulled Bridger and Fitzgerald in over their heads. Having agreed, as they thought, to a limited bout with chance, they had watched it stack the odds against them for days where they had been steeled to outface hours only.

But quitting in itself was not the bad part of the business. Fitzgerald's urge to throw up an undertaking whose demands had proved excessive was no more vicious than the decision of a swimmer to save himself, after having made every reasonable effort to help a drowning man. Where the evil lay was the fact that he was unwilling to admit that he had not been game enough to live up to the letter of his contract. And in order to keep from being suspected of failure, he had to propose brutal cover-up measures.

The crux was that white men didn't follow the Indian practice of packaging weapons and other useful personal effects with the dead. Nor did they throw them away. Those in position to gain them, kept them for their own use, or to sell or trade. This was especially true on the frontier. There men far from the points of manufacture, and forever apt to be in need of replacements due to accidents and Indian thievery, were frugal of any windfall.

That was what tripped Fitzgerald. As he shied from reporting to Henry that he had left the cripple he had vowed to stay with, while Glass was still alive, he had to act as he would have done had Hugh actually first died. This meant that he had to propose robbing a helpless colleague as well as abandoning him.

He didn't have to reach far for justification here, either. A man who had proved too weak to stir from his pallet would certainly find no use for a gun, or anything else in the way of equipment, before his overdue death caught up with him. It would thus be no crime to commandeer items which would else be lost to rust, if not first found by Indian enemies.

Young Bridger argued, but the wilting of the older man sapped his own already shaky nervous walls. In spite of his fears, he had been resigned to staying in a spot with but one seen exit. Now that Fitzgerald had shown him another way out, though, it wasn't long before he let himself be talked into doing what expediency ordered.

The two had an auditor, as they talked things over. If Hugh couldn't plead his cause vocally, he did, as he told Yount, manage to rally the strength to make imploring gestures. But men whose spirits were on the run did what they felt they had to, in order to save their reputations as well as their lives.

To keep from being suspected of welching on their commitment, they took from their bedridden comrade everything calculated to insure survival, in case he did beat the odds and claw his way back from death's brink. They took his "possible sack," holder of odds and ends which included the flint and steel with which to make fire. They took his tomahawk, useful for chopping wood as well as cleaving foes. They took his knife, the wilderness man's all-purpose tool and culinary adjunct, as well as sidearm. They took his supply of powder, shot and percussion caps. They took his rifle.

In addition to being money filched from a blind man's cup, that last was a mortal affront. To a frontiersman afield, his rifle was something besides his mainstay on both ends of war and in the field of commissary. It was more even than the prize possession of a man who had few other chattels upon which to cast a fond eye. During much of his time a plainsman's or mountain man's rifle took the place of the companionship denied him by his way of life. The early Westerner didn't travel with dogs, because their barking made them a hazard in hostile Indian country. The bond between horse and man seldom amounted to much, because thievery, warfare and trail attrition caused a constant change of mounts. So the high-headed affection which men yearn to lavish on something was bestowed by the borderer on the gun which was at once ally, pet and up-to-date miracle of industrial progress.

A rifle might be talked to even when human auditors were present, as Ruxton, among others, asserted that Old Bill Williams did. Like the swords of paladins, furthermore, rifles had names. Some, as in the cases of Bill's "Old Fetchem" and Davy Crockett's "Betsy," have been preserved. Unfortunately no one thought to tell in print what Glass called the weapon taken from him by Fitzgerald and Bridger; but one pertinent thing can be inferred from his reaction to the theft. As he had by then become deeply attached to it, the gun could hardly have been a spare one, turned over to him by Ashley after the massacre in which he had been wounded. It must have been a firearm of his personal selection in St. Louis, or of older ownership dating from his Pawnee days, which he had somehow managed to keep while fleeing through water from Arikara fire.

Hugh's strong attachment to the weapon in question was cited by Clark after hearing from Yount on the subject. Of Glass he wrote that, above and beyond his other afflictions, "He had still to morn the loss of his rifle, which he valued above all price."

How strong and lasting rifle fetishism could be is shown by a linked passage in Clark's manuscript. Yount, as the author discovered, still clung to the gun of his choice long after it had ceased to be a warrior's, or pot hunter's, necessity. The prosperous householder in a pacified country confessed, indeed, that he could not sleep unless the weapon was within arm's reach, and that on the rare occasions when he failed to place it there, he felt lost upon awaking without seeing it.

True of Yount in his contentment; triply true of Glass in his misery. Fitzgerald and Bridger might have left him destitute of everything else without returning heat to all but burnt-out ashes. Yet in wreaking the ewe-lamb injury of stealing the gun of Hugh's bosom, his wrongers had put passion back in a broken man who had a moment since been without any driving gears.

Before proceeding, notice should be taken of the fact that up to this point the story of Hugh's bear encounter and its sequel has been based on testimony other than his own. Many besides himself knew that he was a member of the party that walked up the Grand with Major Henry, pursuant to the Arikara siege. They knew that although he had been the bane of Old Ephraim, he had been so clawed and chewed by the furious monster as to make observers sure that recovery was impossible. They knew that an effort to carry him had been given up as painful, to no purpose, for all concerned. They knew that two men, with a bonus to look forward to, had remained with him, while the rest pushed on to the post at the Yellowstone's mouth. And they knew, too, that he had been abandoned by this pair, or as Potts put it, "he was left by the way without any gun."

That was known because his deserters did not meet any of the Indian war parties they had feared, but arrived at Fort Henry — of which Potts was an inmate at the time — a few days after the Major did. So it was known that they had exhibited Hugh's field equipment, and collected the agreed sum for having stayed with Glass until it was certain that he would never have use for hunting gear again.

Semifinally, it was known that the site of the grave which had supposedly been dug for Hugh was high up toward the headwaters of the Grand, as deep in hostile Indian territory as it was far removed from the Missouri. Lastly, it was known that months after he had been accounted dead, he strode out of the wilderness, alone, and rejoined a party of men who by then had moved many leagues up the Yellowstone from the fort at that stream's mouth.

Knowledge of all those things was the common property of numbers of witnesses. Where the testimony of Glass alone must be depended on is the intervening period, and there is everything from positive to strong supporting evidence to back what he said about that.

The positive and keystone fact is that he did escape from a predicament which had piled the chances against his being able to do so enormously high. The question, then, is not if he accomplished a seeming impossibility, but how he did so. As he held a hand which was all deuces of clubs and made it a winning one, any outside party has a choice between believing what Glass said about the matter or making up a theory of his own on the strength of no knowledge.

Though wonderful, Hugh's feat of cheating the ravens is not in the miracle class, the training given him by his past few years considered. It has, to be sure, come down in several versions, but they all agree as to the essential points.

In his helpless rage at being left destitute, as Hugh told Yount, he became delirious. Checking time in lucid intervals, he estimated that this phase of his ordeal lasted four or five days. He was robbed once more in the course of them, for wolves tugged off the robe with which he had been covered when abandoned, though that vision may have been stamped on his memory by a quirk of fever dreaming.

By the same token, Glass may not have been as aware of the actual moment of desertion as he later recalled. In justice to Bridger and Fitzgerald, the chance should be put forward that an invalid's burst of fury was followed by a lapse into coma which made him appear to be going down for the last time.

But if that was the case, he emerged with a burning mind again. Fever, though, can be a sign of a body struggling to heal itself; and when his brain finally cleared, he found himself stronger than he had been, pitiful as the achievements which proved it might seem.

The one thing which Fitzgerald and Bridger had done for him was to move his pallet close to the spring by which the three had been encamped. Stretching out an arm, Hugh could scoop up water enough to moisten fever-dried lips. He could also reach the buffalo berries which dangled from overhanging bushes. Crushed to a pulp and further softened by water, these could be worked past his mutilated throat, to hold starvation off.

Meanwhile, Hugh wasn't content with merely not

dying. He meant to get out of the fifth-act-curtain fix he was in, kill the men who had left him to fade away in solitude, and regain his precious rifle. Whether or not he ever breathed the formal oath of vengeance ascribed to him by Cooke, he meant nothing but business; and the healthy pursuit of looking past his misery was Hugh's most remarkable accomplishment. Confident, with never a right to be, he never gave morbid thoughts a chance to get in cahoots with his weakness and pull the house down.

But even magnificent self-sureness couldn't squeeze the strength to get moving out of such provender as water-soaked berries. He had to stay where he was, for several more days, abiding the change of fortune of which he told Yount.

Hugh's gift from the gods was one which wouldn't have cheered men more fortunately placed. Upon waking from a nap, he was pleased to see what Clark described as a "very thick" rattlesnake. It was, of course, bulky because it had just swallowed some small animal or fair-sized bird; and like any such recently fed reptile, it was in a state of torpor.

Glass was therefore able to bring a sharp stone to bear upon the neck of a creature helpless to dodge, let alone coil for striking. Doggedly sawing away, he detached the venomous head from several feet of trunk, itself offering a supply of flesh to a man in desperate need of some form of solid nourishment. Because of his ailing throat, though, he had to down raw ophidian by the method pursued in eating buffalo berries. He shredded the meat by grinding it between stones, that is to say, and made a cold stew of it by soaking each mouthful in water.

It is possible that he may have had the aid of a piece of kitchenware when preparing this dish. A couple of accounts say that Bridger and Fitzgerald hadn't bothered to take away a utensil described by Flagg as "a small brass kettle." Agreeing upon this, Cooke and Flagg also say that Glass found an old straight razor in what was variously styled a "wallet" and an otherwise emptied "shot pouch."

But that's the maximum equipment allowed him by any of the accounts, and he couldn't have been able to take the kettle along when he left the spot, because of his means of locomotion. For when the digested rattlesnake gave him the strength to leave his pallet, he found that, although he couldn't rise to walk, he could crawl.

Having made this discovery, he began going after the two men who had stolen his rifle in order to keep from being found out as welchers. Yet the lay of the land forced him to begin by moving away from their line of march when leaving the same place.

After reaching the headwaters of the Grand, Fitzgerald and Bridger had followed the trail of Henry's party over intervening rough country to a tributary of the Little Missouri. But Glass couldn't buck any uphill grades, and as a maimed quadruped he had to stay close to a sure water supply. Realizing this, he commenced creeping back toward the Missouri proper.

5

∧∙∧∙∧∙∧∙∧

The Adventures of a Nemesis

*The Skin boat I saw on the sand bar was made by
four men who crossed over from the mouth of the
Bighorn thier winter camp and landing on the shore
walked up into the village which proved to be Aricka-
rees two of them escaped but the other two were
killed.*

— REMINISCENCES OF JAMES CLYMAN

THE NEAR-SLAYING of Hugh Glass by a grizzly
was not long the last of the string of Western-style
disasters which befell Andrew Henry and those who
continued inside his evil nimbus. After he had left
two hale men with what he deemed a sped one, the
Major found bad news in waiting at the post which he
had been so anxious to reach.

So much can be said on the authority of Black Harris, who later told a reporter of the *Missouri Intelligencer* what the Major learned: "When the party arrived at the mouth of the Yellow Stone, they found that
22 horses had been stolen by the Blackfeet . . . Losing
seven more shortly afterwards, they determined to

abandon that establishment, and ascend the Yellow Stone to the mouth of Powder River . . ."

Finding the ascent of that stream blocked to boatmen by a falls, this division of Ashley's men bought replacement mounts from the Crows, and went on up the Yellowstone toward its confluence with what Potts, in one of his letters, called the "Brighorn." With icicle weather nearing, the Major was anxious to find a suitable spot on which to erect a new trading station. After some peering about, he found a site which took his fancy, and the third house of misfortune known as Fort Henry was built.

While the date of laying its cottonwood cornerstone has not been recorded, the men who did it must have been on their way toward the Big Horn, while Hugh was packing his dozen or so grievous wounds away from the spring, and down the creek of which it was the source, to the Grand. That must have taken place during the first week of 1823's September.

West on the Yellowstone, in the meantime, the two men whom he meant to slay were known as the pair who had had the sand to stick with a dying comrade, and risks be damned. While tradition is silent as to how Fitzgerald carried his honors, it has ascribed to Bridger a gnawing uneasiness, because of having let himself be talked into a course with shameful sequels. Once having agreed to something at odds with his sense of decency, he had become party to a robbery, in order to cover up. For the same purpose, as refusal would have wrinkled suspicious brows, he had had to take money which reminded him of a deserted invalid every time it jingled.

The one consoling pearl in a bad oyster turned out to be a Tecla. Still, it was thought real at the time, and it charmed away the fear that others would know as much as his conscience did, by repeating an old saw. "Dead men tell no tales," was its soothing tenor.

Aside from being unreliable — for the dead have often been apt reporters — this bit of folk wisdom didn't apply. It would have horrified young Bridger to see frustrated buzzards wheeling above a man who propelled himself by one arm and a leg, moving through thickets and tall grass with the painful doggedness of an angleworm bucking dry sand.

At first a day's march was measured in rods, not miles, and not many at that. Another man might have found this a discouraging rate of progress toward his immediate goal. Fort Kiowa was, as Hall pointed out, "a trading establishment on the Missouri River, about three hundred and fifty miles distant." He was counting on covering nearly one hundred and twenty leagues, in a word, and he was commencing with stints of perhaps fifty yards.

While so proceeding, he was less well fixed for worldly goods than he had been back in the grove where he had left his pallet and kettle. When he rested for the night, there was nothing between his mutilated body and the ground but ripped buckskin and dirty rags, black with old blood. If the night was cold, so was he. If it rained at any time, he endured the fingering of his wounds; and again when the high winds of the Great Plains rushed his way.

There was always a chance of meeting hostile Indians, or another grizzly bear. For such contingencies he was armed with a razor he couldn't rise to wield.

He was dismayed neither by these matters nor a commissary problem to daunt hale men. And even well hunters armed with guns, so chancy a place to live was the West of that day, sometimes found less to shoot than Tartarin de Tarascon on the days when he didn't happen to catch a glimpse of Jacques, or was it Pierre?

Daniel Potts was among those who saw the time when men hopeful of buffalo would have been glad to settle for even a small French rabbit:

"We . . . arrived at Cederfort about the middle of July when we were reduced to the sad necessity of eating anything we could cetch as our provision where exausted and no game to be had, being advanced five hundred miles above the fronteers, we were glad to get a Dog to eat and I have seen some geather the skins of Dogs up through the Camp sing[e] and roast them and eat heartyly this so discouraged me that I was determined to turn tail up stream and bear my cours down. . . ."

But Potts, as he related, was to see the time when dogs, if not their skins, would have seemed fancy fare:

"And by the way lost from the others without gun aminition provision or even cloths to my back of much

[?; word blurred] account being four hundred miles from aney white people or even knowing where to find Indians; now my dear friend how must I have felt young Birds, frogs, and Snakes where exceptable food with me and not means of fire . . ."

But leaving out the hardly repeatable luck of finding a torpid reptile Hugh Glass couldn't catch any young birds, frogs and snakes. Nor could he, as Jim Clyman did when pinched and out of ammunition, run badgers down and slay them with the bones of a wild horse.

Yet Hugh had other things to eat than such berries as he could reach, as Clark learned from George Yount: "With sharp stones he would dig from the earth nourishing roots which he had learned to discriminate while sojourning with the Paunees." Yount also told of another dietary dodge which Glass had picked up while living as an Indian. Running across a dead buffalo, its skeleton as yet green enough to contain marrow, Hugh would crack the bones with a rock. Then, after scraping out the rich food matter inside, he would mix it with buffalo berries and emerge with a digestible and strengthening form of nourishment.

So much for science. He also had one really fine piece of luck, this time featuring a live buffalo.

While differing as to when it took place, all the main versions agree upon the central fact. Wolves, which had succeeded in cutting a bison calf out of a herd, chased it to within a few yards of Hugh, before they were able to bring it to earth. While agreeing, too, that Glass managed to become possessed of the pack's kill, the writers voice separate views as to how he did it.

Hall's account is at once the briefest and the least probable, assuming as it does that a man unable to stand could shoo wolves away from their prey, as though they were so many flies that had swooped on a puddle of spilled beer:

"It required no ordinary portion of fortitude to crawl to the end of such a journey through a hostile country, without fire-arms, with scarcely strength to drag one limb after another, and with almost no other substance than wild berries. He had, however, the good fortune to be 'in at the death of a buffaloe calf' which was overtaken and slain by a pack of wolves. He permitted the assailants to carry on the war until no signs of life remained in their victim, and then interfered and took possession of the 'fatted calf;' but as he had no means of striking fire, we may infer that he did not make a very *prodigal* use of the veal thus obtained."

James Hall knew more about the Bible, as his obtrusive pun suggests, than he did about the dietary habits of hungry frontiersmen. To rerun a quote from Potts, "Young Birds, frogs and Snakes where exceptable food with me and not means of fire." Then the Plains tribes, including the one which had counted Hugh as a member, considered the raw entrails of a freshly killed buffalo a treat; and with special relish they would guzzle the yards of small intestine.

So Glass would not have scorned the best food which he had run across merely because he had no means of cooking it. And according to Flagg, at least, he was so far from being short of the means of starting a kitchen blaze that fire reached the calf before he did:

". . . He was roused by a rustling in the bushes, and, on looking around, he saw a small Buffalo-calf approaching at full speed with several wolves in chace. Rising suddenly from his resting place, the calf was driven back upon its pursuers and was immediately slain. He then advanced toward the wolves, but finding that he could no way intimidate them to give up their prize, he produced his razor, and by the aid of a flint and a few dry leaves, set fire to the grass. This manoeuvre was successful — the wolves were put to flight, and nearly the whole of the calf fell into his hands."

While ingenious, and not at all impossible, this method of hijacking Gray Brother's kill does not seem as probable as Cooke's report of what happened: ". . . He witnessed near him the destruction of a buffalo calf by wolves; — and here he gave a proof of cool judgment: he felt certain that an attempt to drive the wolves from their prey before their hunger was at least somewhat appeased, would be attended with danger, and he concluded to wait until they had devoured about half of it, when he was successful in depriving them of the remainder."

Although he may have had to resort to the use of fire, it is clear from all the cited accounts that he had first tried to scare the wolves away by a simpler, if far more dangerous course of action. He had crawled toward them, armed with either his razor or a stick. And whichever weapon he chose, it was feebly flourished by his game hand; the other was used for pushing himself forward.

He didn't have a man's usual advantage of being able to tower over the wolves. He had to meet them on their own quadruped level. If they had jumped him, they could easily have finished what the white bear had begun. But they didn't, and in one fashion or another, he ended up with their prize.

So Hugh had at least half of a calf, dropped perhaps in April, and this was September. Presumably the wolves beat him to it, so he could not have begun, Indian-style, by guzzling the raw liver. Yet if the beasts had gobbled the most easily seized portions, they had performed the service of partially skinning the animal, leaving Glass free to batten on flesh tender enough for his convalescent throat.

The abiding need of one who had lost as much blood as Old Ephraim had let out of Hugh was food with bottom enough to put it back. Dripping with gore, the chunks he ripped from the young buffalo were just behind a blood transfusion in the immediacy with which they joined forces with his system. With his arteries flush for the first time since his terrible encounter, he was now on the way to rising from all fours.

Miraculously, he had improved while denying himself the rest supposedly indispensable to a graveside case. Except for a festering back wound, which he couldn't get at and clean out, the great rents in his body were mending, in spite of the fact that the energies needed for healing had so largely been diverted to the uses of creeping forward. This he had done at a progressively faster rate — so that he was reeling off marches of two miles a day even before the wolves gave him this chance to get off his hands and knees.

Curbing his urge to press toward vengeance, he had the wisdom to stay still and take on more fuel. As torpid as the full rattler he had killed earlier, he rested beside the buffalo carcase and let the food he intermittently wrenched from it renew him.

When he left what remained of the calf a few days later, the odds against him had immeasurably decreased. He was not only over the hump of recovery, he was *Homo erectus* with all the versatility belonging to that state of being. He could watch for Indians and bears, as he could not while a plantigrade animal making his way through grass and shrubbery taller than he. And any young birds, frogs and snakes that he now encountered had better beware. For he could wield a club and heave a throwing stick at these, or any rabbit or badger met along the way.

As for the Missouri, he was, barring further accident, as good as there. The starveling who could crawl a scant two miles a day had been replaced by a walking man who could cover that much in an hour. And his pace quickened with every sun which saw his torn muscles better knitted by his renewed bloodstream.

There was still the problem of his back wound, which alone was not doing well, due to his inability to keep it free of infection, and the creatures that fed on it, when allowed to. The yen for vengeance which was pecking at his brain, though, was as healthy as such

mental churnings are supposed not to be. It and a kind-
lier piston left him no time for the self-concern normal
to prolonged loneliness. He was too busy pressing forward, under the compulsions of hate for two faithless
men, and love for the rifle carried off by one of them.

Flagg and Cooke wrote that Hugh did at length meet
Indians: a band of Sioux traveling as a village on the
march, and not as a war party. Domestic of mood,
they took a kindly interest in one who showed so many
signs of having lately tangled with the foe most respected by the savages of the Plains.

Although Flagg stated that this occurred before
Hugh reached the Missouri, the odds favor Cooke's assertion that Glass met the Dakotas after his arrival
(during the first few days in October) at what fire had
left of the Arikara villages. As these lay north of the
Grand by eight miles, they didn't stand along the short-
est road to Fort Kiowa. Yet if Cooke was vague as to
why Hugh took this detour, several reports of tangent
Sioux maneuvers make it understandable.

Arch foes of the Rees, the Dakotas were said
to have returned for repeated harvestings of Arikara
farm products, as various kinds of corn, and other
plantings of the fled tribe, ripened. Undoubtedly, the
Indians Glass encountered were on their way to make
another agricultural raid.

Hugh, in the meantime, had found this side trip
worthwhile on another count. Cooke declared that his
tramp to the empty villages was rewarded by the discovery of some dogs which hadn't joined their fleeing
Ree masters, and that Glass was able to lure one of

/   147

these within throat-cutting range. Next, butchering the
animal with the razor used in executing it, he was able
to enjoy what many plainsmen came to join Indians
in considering the meat of meats.

It was after this go at being a gourmet that he met
some of the Dakotas haunting the vicinity. On his way
downriver toward Fort Kiowa, "he was discovered by a
small party of Sioux Indians: these acted toward him
the part of the good Samaritan. The wound on his back
was found in a horrid condition. It had become full of
worms! The Indians carefully washed it and applied
an astringent vegetable liquid."

In concurring with Cooke, Flagg declared that Hugh
"fell into the hands of a band of Sioux Indians. Com-
passionating his defenseless and miserable condition,
the savages received him kindly, and afforded him safe
conduct to the French trading post, Lesau."

When learning the story himself, Flagg's informant
didn't get the name of this trading station quite straight.
Actually it was called "Fort Brazeau" when it wasn't, to
the bewilderment of many a historian, styled "Fort Lookout" or "Fort Kiowa." Chroniclers who have understood
the identity of the last two haven't linked them to the
first for lack of knowing the nickname, which the elder
of the two fur traders named Brazeau brought west
from Kaskaskia, Illinois. Whatever the Indian word
meant, "Cayewa" junior inherited this nickname from
"Cayewa" senior; and it was Americanized as Kiowa,
to bring it in line with the name of a Southwestern
tribe never known to have ever dwelt near the Upper
Missouri.

Whether the Sioux put Glass a-horseback or conveyed him downstream in the buffaloskin coracle known as a "bullboat," he could have reached Fort Kiowa within a few days of his departure from the Ree villages. There was a nearer post or so — Fort Teton, near the mouth of the Bad, for one — but Hugh had had an excellent reason for choosing as his goal the particular station he did.

Fort Kiowa was where Ashley and those with him had gone, after parting from Andrew Henry's crew at the mouth of the Grand. As the post which the General was using as his headquarters, this fort was the one where Hugh could count on getting, via jawbone, the equipment with which to go after Fitzgerald and Bridger in better style, and with the weapons he needed, in order to do away with them.

Arriving not later than October 11, Hugh missed Ashley by less than two weeks. After long deliberation, the General had decided to launch an expedition which had no connection with the plans of the Rocky Mountain Fur Company as originally worked out by Major Henry and himself. Although he hadn't yet heard that the Blackfeet had forced Henry to drop the scheme of pushing up to the Missouri's headwaters, Ashley had lost all faith in the big river's usefulness to the fur trade, following the Arikara siege fiasco.

On September 29 he had finally played the chip which was to have the effect of shifting the main locus of trapping from the Plains to the Rockies, and the Great Basin beyond them. That is as much as to say that he had named Jed Smith captain of a party which included Jim Clyman, Tom Fitzpatrick and Bill Sublette, while Ed Rose had contracted to go part of the way in the role of interpreter. Heading down the Missouri as far as the White River, they had ridden up along this stream, bound for the Black Hills and other parts of which nothing was known to the men of the Missouri.

Knowing he could afford no other gamble in the fur trade unless this one paid off, Ashley had left for St. Louis on the next pirogue, or Mackinaw boat, steering in that direction. But as the General's credit was good at Fort Kiowa, a destitute Ashley man could re-equip himself there.

Now, between the time of his abandonment and that of his arrival at Fort Brazeau, Glass was naturally the sole original narrator — and never mind the arguing echoes of what he said — of his experiences, while getting from and to places some 350 miles apart. But once at this station, he was where his hidden activities could be checked against what he did, under the spotlight.

A less driven man might have felt that he deserved a respite, after winning to safety in defiance of such handicaps as had hemmed him in; but Hugh had to see some fellows about a gun. He couldn't have been at Cayewa Brazeau's post more than a couple of days before he stepped aboard a craft with its prow pointed upstream toward the Yellowstone.

After the massacre of Ashley's second expedition by

the Rees, the Mandans had been in the state of excitement which found its outlet in the attack on Henry's party, of which Hugh himself had been a member. Probably the wilderness wireless network had carried news of that engagement; but at all events most traders had kept away from a tribe reported as no longer safe to deal with.

By October, however, things were as they had been in Mandanland, with one exception. After wandering no one has said whither for some weeks, the Rees had found a place to light. As the *Missouri Intelligencer* later observed, with Black Harris for authority, "The Aricarees have purchased a dirt village one mile below the Mandans, which they inhabit."

But the cooled-off Mandans had made one stipulation when agreeing to this arrangement. They told the burned-out Rees they didn't want the commission of any acts which might draw white arsonists to their villages, too. Chastened by their need of the time being, most of the Arikaras consented to bury their hatchets elsewhere than in paleface skulls; but the band once led by Grey Eyes, the cannon-beheaded, refused to swallow their hatred for the people who had made them homeless. Wrathful with the appeasers who stayed, they rode off under the leadership of Elk's Tongue, telling none where they were going.

When news of these matters drifted down the river, Joseph Brazeau reasoned that it would be safe to send a trading deputation to the two tribal neighbors. "Cayewa" didn't go himself, but handed the leadership to Antoine Citoleux, who also had a nickname. In his case it was so tenacious that most chronicles refer to him only as "Langevin."

On October 10, or not much later, the man of this *nom de guerre* left Fort Kiowa. The vessel he commanded could have been the pirogue, or dugout canoe, cited in some accounts, but in all likelihood it was the Mackinaw boat mentioned in others. Such a craft was propelled by a couple of pairs of oars, though it could be sailed when the wind was obliging.

Of the six men aboard, the names of two besides Langevin are worth noting. One was Toussaint Charbonnau, the interpreter whom Colonel Leavenworth had vainly sent in pursuit of the Arikaras, with a plea to return to their villages. The other was Hugh Glass.

While Yount was vague as to the makeup of this expedition, the other three are more specific. Hugh, as Flagg noted after bringing Glass as far as the trading post he called Lesau, decided to join "a party of seven traders being about to start for the Mandan Villages in a *pirogue*, he was received by them, and was once more en route."

Having brought Hugh safely to "Fort Kiawa," to use Hall's spelling, his version went on as follows:

"Before his wounds were entirely healed, the chivalry of Glass was awakened, and he joined a party of five engages, who were bound, in a pirogue, to Yellow Stone River. The primary object of this voyage was declared to be the recovery of his arms, and vengeance on the recreants who had robbed and abandoned him in his hour of peril."

While Cooke didn't know where the party started from — he had brought Hugh to a post by the mouth of the Bad, which would have been Fort Teton — he knew, even if he misspelled, the name of its leader:

"A party of six of the engages, headed by one Longevan, had occasion about this time to ascend the Missouri in a Mackinaw, with the purpose of trading with the Mandans about three hundred miles above: these Glass decided to accompany . . . His great object, it may be readily conjectured, was to meet the two wretches he was so much indebted to."

None of these narrators knew the date of departure, but that can be fixed with near accuracy because of an odd development. Although obeying Brazeau's orders to go among the Mandans and Rees, Langevin became fey; and while foreboding didn't cause him to turn back to safety, it led him to make his will. This he did upon reaching Simoneau Island, fifteen miles south of Bad River's junction with the Missouri, and left it with traders stationed there. As that document was preserved, the date when it was drawn up is a matter of record.

Antoine Citoleux, *autrement dit* Langevin, made his last will and testament on Simoneau Island on October 15, 1823. By those who understand the mileage to be expected of a hand-powered craft, opposing the Missouri's current in that part of the river and in that season, it has been estimated that it must have taken the group Hugh was with four or five days to get from Fort

/ 153

Kiowa to where their leader arranged to dispose of his worldly goods.

The farther they went, next, the slower they fared. As they were rowing or paddling uphill, the water the Missouri poured down did so with ever-increasing force. Then they were surging north and northwest at a time of the year when winds from those compass points pushed against their bow and added waves to the current they were fighting. It was cold boating, too, for November lay in wait behind October, and beyond South Dakota was the northern twin. There summers are short, and fall is often hard to tell from a winter with a name for fierceness. So, what with one thing and another, it has been judged that the French *voyageurs* and their American passenger were six weeks in transit.

Throwing his mind past the Mandans, Hugh meanwhile was thinking of what he would do when he reached the post at the mouth of the Yellowstone. As no messengers had recently come down the Missouri from that vicinity, it was still not known that the Major had moved, first, as far up the Yellowstone as the Powder — stretching the trail ahead of Hugh by over forty leagues.

After reporting that much to the *Missouri Intelligencer*, Black Harris had had more to say. With some of the forty-seven horses bought from the Crows, to replace the ones lifted by Blackfeet, the Major had mounted a westward-ordered field party. He had, moreover, given Glass another one hundred miles to travel by choosing to build his new fort near the mouth of the Big Horn.

That statement was a misleading one, doubtless owing to the newspaper reporter's failure to get his facts straight. Trusting him, scholarly investigators have vainly looked for traces, above or below the Big Horn, which would enable them to fix the precise site of this station. But in his letter of 1824, Potts said it wasn't along the Yellowstone at all. "From thence," he wrote, with reference to the fort on the Missouri, "we moved our cours for the mouth of the little horn."

As this tributary of the Big Horn joins the latter thirty miles short of the Yellowstone, the men Hugh was stalking were eighty or so leagues farther off than he thought to be the case. Not for many days, though; at least, both of them didn't stick it out where Major Andrew Henry found no better luck than he had in the past. It is possible that Black Harris left the post on orders from Henry. What seems more likely — and this has been stated — is that he and two more tired of a leader with whom every day was Friday the thirteenth, and so mustered themselves out of his command.

One of the pair who left with Harris is without face or name, but the other was John S. Fitzgerald. And when he stowed his gear in the skiff which was to take the trio back to the Missouri and eastward down that river, it included a rifle filched from a man who meant to get it back.

Harris, Fitzgerald and the other started in mid-November, by which time Hugh and his companions had been weeks on the water. Although Fort Henry was farther away from the Mandan villages than was Brazeau's fort, the difference between going with strong rivers and pulling against one was comparable to the space between coasting down a slope and trudging back up it, bobsled in tow.

Working at closing the interval at separate wet ends of it, in brief, the slow-moving hunter and his speeding prey were bound for the same stopping-point on or about November 20. As it turned out, though, Fitzgerald was a few days late in arriving, while Glass, for a time, was given something to think of beside his gun and the pair that had walked off with it.

The episode can suitably be introduced by what the *St. Louis Enquirer* had to say about the Rees: "It now appears that after they fled from their Villages, the Arikarees sought the protection of the Mandans and obtained it on the promise of future friendly deportment toward the whites — that this was promised by all except a small band who breathe nothing but vengeance, and separated themselves from the main body."

Had Elk's Tongue and his followers stayed in the vicinity, they would have seen no grounds for their secession. If there were any reformed characters among the redskins of the Plains, they weren't Arikaras. They proved as much at a site identified by Prince Maximilian of Wied as the mouth of the Cannon Ball.

Five or six men belonging to Mr. Brazeau's trading establishment were lately killed near the Aricara Village, [the *Missouri Intelligencer* announced, when it finally got

word of the event]. They were finally conveyed in a bat-
teau, and were going up for the purpose of trading with the
Mandans and Aricaras. Within one day's voyage of the
Aricara village, the patroon, apprehensive of danger, left
his company and proceeded by land. He promised to re-
join them at the Mandans, whose town, one mile above
the Aricaras, he entered under cover of night. The day after
his arrival, he received the news that his men were all
murdered, his cargo captured, and his boat sunk.

Actually the man whose caution thus saved him was
not the "patroon," who was Langevin, but Toussaint
Charbonnau, who lived for many years to come. Fey
though he was, Langevin could not have told his men
to go by day whither he preferred to tiptoe in the dark,
and historically he went down near, if not actually
with, his rowed or paddled ship.

Hugh Glass was the party's other survivor, but not
because he stole a march on trouble, or even suspected
its presence. When the sun came up behind Charbonnau's furtive departure, the rest followed the river as
far as the start of a lengthy bend, by whose upstream
end the Mandan villages stood. At this point Hugh was
put ashore — the authorities standing two and two as
to why this was done.

Yount said that Glass preferred the overland short-
cut to the roundabout water route, and that statement
could look to two counts for support. Aside from the
patent fact that walking must have been more comfort-
able than sitting in a boat, at that season, Hugh's business was not trading with the Mandans but pressing on
toward the Yellowstone's mouth. He could have saved a

day in travel time by not waiting for the others to make the long pull around the bend, and he could very well have chosen to do this.

Something of the sort can be read in Hall's narrative:

"When the party had ascended to within a few miles of the old Mandan village, our trapper, of hair breadth 'scapes, landed for the purpose of proceeding to Tilton's Fort at that place, by a nearer route than that of the river. On the following day, all the companions of his voyage were massacred by the Arickara Indians."

Well and good; but Flagg implied that Hugh was set ashore to hunt for the crowd, and Cooke also declared that this was the case:

"Late in an afternoon, at this time, they unsuspectingly landed to put ashore a hunter; and as it happened, at a point nearly opposite the spot chosen by the Arickaras for their temporary abode. Ever on the alert, the boat-full of white men had early been descried by one of their out parties. So all was in readiness for the unconscious objects of savage revenge. — Scarce had the boat grated on the beach, and Glass as the hunter, (his lucky star still prevailing) gained the concealment of willows, than a hundred guns, a hundred bows sent forth their fatal missiles; — and on the instant — the shrill war cry from a thousand mouths . . .

"But few guns from the boat sent back defiance to the murderous discharge; the shouts were but answered by the death cry and expiring groans. The Indians rushed upon their victims, and the war club and tomahawk finished a work that had been so fearfully begun."

In all but Cooke's account, nonetheless, Glass is shown as being miles away when the attack on Langevin's crew bloodied the right bank of the Missouri; and they agree that Hugh didn't know Ree guns were loaded for palefaces until he neared the village of the warriors to whom he was already indebted for one wound.

"He had proceeded but a few miles," Flagg wrote, "when he came upon a roving band of Erickeraw Indians, who chanced to have there an encampment, and a party of them, as soon as he was perceived, gave chace, evidently with hostile designs. The savages gained upon the hunter rapidly, and he would undoubtedly have been seized and butchered, had not an Indian of the Mandan tribe, who was hovering on a fleet horse around the encampment, perceived his danger, and, at great personal hazard galloping up to him across the prairie, succeeded in taking him off from his pursuers. — On arriving at the Mandan villages Glass learned to his horror, that his seven companions in the *pirogue* had been seized by the Erickeraws, and every soul of them murdered!"

Yount told Clark that Hugh was first seen by some Arikara squaws, out gathering firewood. In response to their shrieks that a white man was in the vicinity, a number of braves mounted for a chase that would have been successful, had not a pair of Mandans seen a chance to gain glory by robbing the Rees of their victim elect. Jumping on their ponies, they dashed gleefully forth, scooped Glass up and scampered back to their village, followed by Arikaran howls of disgust.

While saying much the same thing, Hall stated that Hugh was taken to a nearby post of the Columbia Fur Company (which the writer had begun by giving as the latter's destination, when Glass was set ashore by Langevin and his crew): "Approaching the fort with some caution, he observed two squaws whom he recognized as Arickaras, and who, discovering him at the same time, turned and fled. . . . The squaws were not long in rallying the warriors of the tribe, who immediately commenced the pursuit. Suffering still under the severity of his recent wounds, the poor fugitive made but a feeble essay at flight, and his enemies were within rifle shot of him, when two Mandan mounted warriors rushed forward and seized him. Instead of despatching their prisoner, as he had anticipated, they mounted him on a fleet horse, which they had brought out for that purpose, and carried him into Tilton's Fort without injury."

That split-second rescue shows up in Cooke's version, too, though as the climax of a longer tale. According to him, be it remembered, Glass had left the beached Mackinaw boat just before the Rees loosed their volley at that target. The thick bottomland brush enabled Hugh to steal from the vicinity unseen, but only to find himself cut off:

"Glass had thus far escaped a cruel fate. He had gained the almost impervious concealment of drifted and matted willows, when the dread ebullition of triumph and death announced to him the evil he had escaped and his still imminent peril. Like the hunted fox, he doubled, he turned, ran or crawled, successively gaining the various concealments of the dense bottom to increase his distance from the bloody scene. And such was his success, that he had thought himself nearly safe, when at a slight opening he was suddenly faced by a foe. It was an Arikara scout . . ."

Taken by itself the duel that followed would not be suspect, but sandwiched between two other near-mortal misses, it has the look — as does nothing else in any of the versions — of deliberate high-piling. Not by Cooke himself, for he was a ramrod of uprightness, loathed by many a superior officer for his refusal to bend. But it would certainly seem that, before the story reached his ears, somebody threw something in for the fun of it, whereas the other changes rung by the sundry accounts appear nothing more than the normal variants of a story which has been sifted through a spread of memories. And different reasoning processes naturally played a part; for whenever recollection dropped a stitch or so, the narrator would as inevitably tend to patch, by guessing how Hugh met this or that known situation.

With the exception of this one all episodes found in any of the versions are as functional as motor parts; they are all needed by the respective narratives to show how Glass fell in and scrambled out of hot water, or how he got to be where he was at the time. But this isn't functional. It doesn't explain how Hugh slipped by his real obstacle, which was not merely one Indian but the whole vindictive Arikara tribe.

Yet as Cooke has been consulted on so many other points, he can't be dismissed without a hearing now. Having brought Glass and the Ree brave together, he proceeded:

". . . So close were these wily woodsmen that but the one had scarce time to use a weapon intended for a much greater distance. The deadly tomahawk of the other was most readily substituted for the steeled arrow. At the instant, it flew through the air, and the rifle was discharged; neither could see or feel the effect produced, but they rushed to each other's grasp, either endeavouring to crush his adversary by the shock of the onset. . . . But Glass, not wholly recovered from his wounds, was doomed to sink beneath the superior strength of his adversary, by an irresistible effort of which he was rolled upon the earth, the Indian above."

But it was a blood-covered Indian; and all in all it's hard to keep from wondering whether this combat didn't originate in the brain of Sir Walter Scott, who had described one marvelously like it in *The Lady of the Lake*:

> They tug, they strain! Down, down they go,
> The Gael above, Fitz-James below.

But before being thrown by Roderick Dhu, Scotland's disguised king had wielded a rapier, which had repeatedly let out blood belonging to the wild Highlander. So just as Clan Alpine's chief was getting set to polish

Fitz-James off with a dirk, Roderick collapsed instead.

As Scott's narrative poem was first published in 1810, it could logically have inspired the ensuing parallel:

"And here his [Hugh's] career would probably have closed; but that in truth it seemed that he bore a charmed existence. At this instant the effect of his unerring shot developed. The Indian's last convulsive exertion, so successful, was accompanied by a shout of victory — but expiring on his lips, it marked his soul's departure. . . . Redeemed, unhoped, from death, Glass beheld at his feet his late enemy, not only dead, but already stiffening, with one hand instinctively touching the hilt of his knife."

But whether true or a borrowing from a then very popular verse romance, the incident still left Glass short of a haven. In telling how he reached one, Cooke wrote much to the same effect as his fellow authorities. Sighted by Rees, Hugh was making a poor race of it against their horses, when a single mounted Mandan (as in Flagg's version) cut in on the run and carried him to his village. There, Cooke concluded, "Glass was well received, for the announcement of his presence was naturally accompanied by the story of his escapes, which naught but the greatest bravery could have accomplished; and nothing is better calculated effectually to engage the interest and admiration of Indians."

Undoubtedly this was true, and almost as certainly tribal versions, or parts of them, were among those eventually picked up and included in the Hugh Glass cycle. Cooke's statement checks with Neihardt's discovery that Hugh's story was a tradition preserved by prairie Indians, as well as white old-timers of the region, as late as the twentieth century's first decade. Of course, the Mandans were pleased to find that the paleface rescued by one or a pair of their braves bore the signs of an even rougher bout with adventure; signs which had earlier stirred the curiosity of the red and white men met by Glass at Fort Kiowa and the intervening posts. While the wounds given him by Old Ephraim were still in the process of healing, the man who met a bear began to be the talk of the Plains; and interest in him deepened when the grapevine began spreading tales of how he'd again played the greased pig that death couldn't hold.

The Mandans were not the only ones in a position to tell at first hand how Hugh had twice escaped the Rees. Toussaint Charbonnau was in one of the villages at the time, and near at hand were William P. Tilton and other inmates of the Columbia Fur Company station named in his honor. Like the adjacent Indian log-and-mud villages, the fort squatted west of the Missouri, near the site of modern Mandan, South Dakota.

If Glass wasn't first taken to this post, as Hall said was the case, he doubtless visited it — secondly to be sociable, but primarily to see if there was any chance of catching a Yellowstone-bound boat. There was none. For reasons given by Prince Maximilian, the traders Hugh questioned were then not troubled by wanderlust:

"The garrison of the fort built by Mr. [James] Kipp consisted of only five men, beside Mr. Tilton the director. It was, therefore, in constant danger because of the near vicinity of the Arikkaras. Those savages remained constantly close to the fort: one of their chiefs, Stanapat (the little hawk with the bloody hand) killed one of Mr. Tilton's people at the very door of the fort. . . . Neither Messrs Tilton and Kipp nor any of their people durst venture out of the fort, where they were obliged to remain in durance the whole of the autumn."

Maximilian also declared that the Mandans were angry with the Rees for reneging on the contract not to attack white men, a circumstance which no doubt accounted for the willingness of one or two of them to spite the Arikaras by saving Hugh. So neither they nor he, by the token of such a tribal cleft, may have promptly learned of the Ree ambuscade, some leagues down the river. Indeed, if Langevin *et al.* were slain after Glass was out of earshot, it is possible that Hugh didn't learn that he'd almost been a massacre victim until after he left Mandanland.

Hall said that Glass was so bent on ridding the West of two other frontiersmen that he cleared out of Fort Tilton on the day of his arrival. This, as the combined statements of Flagg and Hall show, was about November 20.

Having learned that the Columbia Fur Company men were sweating out a siege, he left in the dark and took the added precaution of having himself ferried to the east bank, then innocent of Rees. But at best his was

/   165

another desperate undertaking. "He was," Flagg observed, "without a solitary companion for this long and perilous journey — his sole conveyance was his feet and his sole defence against savages and wild beasts his rifle: — besides the weather had become severely cold, and snow lay on the frozen soil for the most part of his route a foot in depth! And yet this enterprising man started out undaunted."

If he was leaving the Arikaras behind, he was walking toward the range of the warlike Assiniboin, while his destination was a post he believed to be still harried by Blackfeet. These might be dodged, or not met at all, if luck stayed his friend, but there was no hiding from the cold; and often there was nothing to break gales fresh out of the Arctic. As Cooke pointed out, the country bracketing this section of the Missouri "is nearly bare of timber; the river bottom is narrow and on but one side at a time, changing at intervals of twenty or thirty miles." This meant that if snow blew his way at the wrong time, there was nothing to serve as shelter but withered grass.

The equipment with which Hugh braved savage men and elements is also described by Cooke: "His arms were now a rifle, small axe and the ever necessary knife; his dress a blanket capote (perhaps flannel) shirt, leather leggins and mockasins, and a cap; he was, in addition, equipped with a blanket and a small kettle, composing a bundle appended on his back."

His food he had to find as he advanced, and it was while looking for game, or else cutting across a stretch bridging a bend in the river, that Glass missed the man he most wanted to see. For if he likewise meant to rub out Jim Bridger, he first yearned to snap the lifeline of John Fitzgerald.

Bowled along by a swift current, Fitzgerald, Harris and their boatmate sped down the Missouri and reached Fort Tilton a few days after Hugh had left. Naturally they learned that a man, long billed as dead, had recently visited the post; but it was a subject on which they probably had little to say themselves.

For Fitzgerald, the news stood for his conviction as a contract breaker who'd collected pay on the strength of a lie. While he couldn't have liked the springing of that jack-in-the-box, it improbably made his friends reproach him. Whether the third man had been present, when Andrew Henry called for volunteers to stay with Glass, is one of history's lost dogs. But Black Harris had been there, and Fitzgerald didn't have to remind him that he wasn't one of the ones who had thought so well of a chance to lose his scalp, while keeping a death watch, as to have bid for it.

It seems fairly certain that Harris likewise remembered that he had been chased into a stream by a cub while Hugh was mortally engaged by a grown white bear. Although his urge to avoid even a half-grown grizzly was as normal as five fingers to the hand, the memory of that flight was one that he was unlikely to have cherished.

Sealed with words or understood without them, an agreement to keep silent on one subject must have been among the things they forthwith took down river with them. There was a question now raised by Arikaras, as to whether they would be able to run the whole course. Perhaps the band led by Elk's Tongue, some of the tribe, had temporarily returned to the burned villages straddling Cottonwood Creek. In the upshot the decision was that the old home wasn't salvageable, but while these redmen were still brooding over the ruins the trio of trappers paddled or rowed near.

Expecting to find no Indians there, they were almost in the slot between the towns and the island opposite when they learned of their mistake. In a subsequent discussion of the Rees, the St. Louis *Enquirer* noted that "They have robbed three of Henry's men." The men weren't present at the time of the robbery, though, a point made clear by Maximilian's report: "Three white men coming from the Rocky Mountains were obliged by the Arikkaras, who lay in wait, to abandon their boat and to escape, at immediate risk of their lives, to the opposite shore."

The Rees got everything, probably, except the weapons of the fleeing frontiersmen. But the savages evidently didn't think the skiff or canoe was worth having; for Harris implied that the trappers were able to find their way back to it that night and glide from the vicinity in the dark.

Save for that delay, they made the good time possible when strong arms and a stronger current are driving a light craft. By December 20 they were at Fort Atkinson, across from Council Bluffs. Apprised of the arrival of men from the Yellowstone River region, General Henry Atkinson talked to their spokesman, Black Harris, on that date, and sent a report of his findings to General Edmund P. Gaines.

Leaving out matters involving Hugh Glass, Harris was a thesaurus of information, both at Fort Atkinson and later at St. Louis. He gave the date of the attack on Henry's party by the Mandans and Minitaris, and named the two white men slain then. He told exactly how many horses had been lifted by the Blackfeet in different raids, and so on. But to neither the General nor the *Missouri Intelligencer* did he mention the Ree massacre of Langevin and his men; for then he would have had to tell not only who was killed, but who had survived.

This diffidence on the part of an otherwise talkative man was and is a great loss. Black Harris became one of the most renowned campfire chroniclers of his day. He was of Henry's party when Old Ephraim charged Glass, and he may have even seen that onslaught. He was at the post near the Yellowstone when Fitzgerald and Bridger arrived with the tale of Hugh's death, and the rifle he supposedly no longer needed or wished. He was with Fitzgerald when the latter was punched with the news that Glass hadn't died. Harris could have been *the* authority on the most remarkable episode in Western history; but he lived for twenty-six years more and said — nothing.

Now, while he and Fitzgerald were still on their way to Fort Atkinson, the man they didn't talk about was walking upstream with only low temperatures and high winds for company. The first leg was a journey of three hundred river miles, less whatever shortcuts he could take when the river bent sharply, but plus whatever ground he had to cover while hunting for game.

As the trip was an uneventful one, the accounts take this rugged march through the snow in stride. "In two weeks," to give Cooke's summation, "he reached the mouth of the Yellow Stone, having met with neither white man or Indian; he crossed the Missouri on a raft, made of two logs tied together with bark." In view of the conditions, the journey must have used up more than a fortnight. Hall declared that it took Hugh thirty-eight days to get from Fort Tilton to the new Fort Henry. There is reason to believe that this time allotment is right.

But that can wait in the wings a moment. Although the informants of Cooke and Hall assumed that Glass was aware of Henry's change of base, Hugh can have known no such thing. He didn't find that he had farther to go until he arrived at a deserted post.

Doubtless Henry left some trail marker, showing the general direction taken. That's all that Glass could have had to go on, though, for the Major didn't know that he was going to set his course for the "little horn" when he started up the Yellowstone. All wayside traces being hidden by snow, Hugh might have doubted his ability to track down a party somewhere in a never-before-visited wilderness; but he strode ahead, and toward the last of December — on New Year's Eve itself, according to Yount — he neared the confluence of the major and minor Big Horn rivers.

With Langevin's preserved will as an anchor point, together with the average speed of muscle-powered craft upriver from there, it has — to say it again — been logically established that it took Glass from about October 10 to around November 20 to travel from Fort Kiowa to the Mandan villages. Not only do Yount, Flagg and Hall agree that Hugh covered the next five hundred and fifty miles or so by the end of December, but logic speaks for the interval between departure and arrival posed by Hall.

During that period of almost six weeks he was — as in the case of his lonely progress down the Grand — the only possible source of word as to how he had fared. But as for each trip the facts were different, so was his report of them.

Had Hugh been the taffy-puller of truth postulated by some born a century later, here would have been a chance to loose the wild geese of fancy without fear of being checked on by any bird-bander. No longer a cripple, he could have made himself the hero of der-ring-do unlimited. Yet nothing emerged from a great undertaking but the simplest of accounts. In the face of conditions which would have daunted most, he had set out to find two men who had bereft him; and by perse-verance he had reached the place where he thought they both were.

"Right weary did he become of his journey," as Cooke credibly declared. And Cooke was doubtless right in adding that the cold was beyond anything Glass had heretofore experienced. He had wintered on the Plains before, but high up the Yellowstone he was in mountain country.

Aside from the squints of Cooke and Flagg at what he had to endure, the accounts say nothing until he was again among witnesses, of whom one was Allen "of Mohave notoriety." Allen told Yount that the garrison of Fort Henry was celebrating the passing of 1823, when the revel was killed by the arrival of the next nearest thing to a ghost.

Doubting their liquor then, they first took it for granted that Hugh was a comeback from the grave. In part they recognized him, but his features had been dauntingly altered by Old Ephraim. Nor were they for a time reassured, when he announced his identity, for the wound in his throat had changed his tones to one of strange timbre.

Flagg offered no description of a moment which must have indeed been dramatic, and Hall noted only that Glass was disappointed at not finding Fitzgerald. Cooke, however, more or less echoed Yount, except that he portrayed Hugh as first encountering some hunters sent out from the fort:

"On reaching them, long was it before they could make up their minds to believe their eyes; to believe that it was the same Glass before them, whom they left, as they thought, dying of wounds, and whose expected death was related to them by two witnesses. To them it was a mystery; and belief of the act of black treachery, which could only explain a part of it, was slow in being enforced upon their minds; — and they touched him, to ensure that it was no ghostly deception."

Yet Hugh hadn't come there just to let his former comrades know that he was still alive. While the staring trappers were quizzing him, he was trying to break through their barrage of queries and learn the whereabouts of the two he meant to tell off and cut down:

"Overwhelmed with questions or demands of explanation, it was long before he could ascertain of them in return, that the party had rendezvoused for winter at the Forks, which was but a few miles distant, that Fitzgerald was not there, having deserted; and that the youth was still one of the expedition."

Arrived at the Forks, or where the Little Big Horn joined the Big Horn proper, Hugh at last confronted one of the men who had been on his mind ever since he had begun creeping at the other end of a twelve-hundred-mile journey. But what he saw before him bore no resemblance to the demonic figure of evil etched on his brain by the acid of vintaged wrath. What he beheld was a nineteen-year-old boy, his bulging adam's apple but one of the symptoms that he was still in the sapling stage.

The picture given of Jim Bridger, by both Orange Clark and Cooke, is one of a youth whose troubled conscience had come face to face with a horrifying embodiment of hidden sin, sprung by Hell to exact punishment. If others thought Glass was a revenant, Jim was sure of it, nor was he in doubt as to why the guardians of the afterworld had given Hugh's specter a pass to return to this one.

So frightened that he barely stayed conscious, Bridger couldn't run. Yet neither could Hugh bring himself to war upon a youngster dissolved in dread.

"Glass," Cooke wrote, "was unprepared for such a spectacle; and well was it calculated to create pity; for some moments he could not find words, much less the act of his purpose. He leaned upon his rifle; his thoughts took a sudden turn; the more guilty object of his revenge had escaped; the pitiful being before him was, perhaps, but the unwilling and over persuaded accomplice of his older companion; — these and other thoughts crossed his mind; and he determined upon the revenge which sinks deepest upon minds not wholly depraved, and of which the magnanimous are alone capable; he determined to spare his life."

What Cooke supposed to be the case, Yount affirmed. Hugh, it should be recalled, had told him that he had overheard the discussion leading up to his abandonment, and that Fitzgerald had proposed it and stampeded Bridger into agreeing. In view of this recollection, he decided to take vengeance on the older man alone — but not before saying to Jim words which the Reverend Clark set down as follows:

"Go, my boy, — I leave you to the punishment of your own conscience and your God. If they forgive you, then be happy — I have nothing to say to you — but don't forget hereafter that truth and fidelity are too valuable to be trifled with."

Whether Yount got the seeds of that sermon from

Hugh himself, or from either Allen or Dutton, is not determinable. The version given by Cooke is longer but less homiletic:

"Young man, it is Glass that is before you; the same, that not content with leaving, you thought, to a cruel death upon the prairie, you robbed, helpless as he was, of his rifle, his knife, of all with which he could hope to defend or save himself from famishing in the desert. In case I had died, you left me to despair worse than death, with no being to close my eyes. I swore an oath that I would be revenged on you and the wretch who was with you; and I ever thought to have kept it. For this meeting I have braved the dangers of a long journey; this has supported me in my weary path through the prairie; for this have I crossed raging rivers. But I cannot take your life; I see you repent; you have nothing to fear from me; go, you are free; — for your youth I forgive you."

While the overwhelmed Jim Bridger was being led away by a kindly comrade or so, Hugh hardened his resolve to hunt down the thief of his rifle — and with that, Cooke dropped the tale. Evidently he knew more about Glass, or had reason to believe that he could learn more, because the second installment of his newspaper account of 1830 concludes with the phrase *To be continued.* It wasn't. And when he republished the item in *Scenes and Adventures in the Army* many years later, his version stopped at the same point.

From the arrival of Glass at the post on the Big Horn, accordingly, the story is carried forward by only Hall,

Flagg and Yount. Yet for some weeks after Hugh's interview with Jim, winter kept the former from pursuing his quest for his rifle and the man who had it.

Besides those at Fort Henry, meanwhile, two other parties of Ashley men were forced to mark time by deepening snow, as well as the winds which piled it around tepees and stuffed gulleys with it. One of these was the group which had left Fort Kiowa the previous September under the leadership of Jed Smith, and with Ed Rose for guide. After leaving the White River behind, they had crossed the Black Hills, and thence journeyed something south of west across Wyoming, to where they found an encampment of Crows on the Wind. By then in the shadow of the Rockies, they settled down for a session of tribal life, while waiting for warmer weather to clear a pass and let them across.

The second party had been sent out by Andrew Henry, apparently just after he'd decided where to build a new post. A member of this expedition, Potts referred to it as follows: "From thence we moved our cours for the mouth of the little horn and by the way I was closely pursuid by a party of Indians on Horsback whom I took to be Black feet and narrowly made my escape by hiding in a little brush and they came close that I could see the very whites of their eyes which was within five yards. — from thence I started with 7 others a traping accross the Rocky Mountains at the commencement of winter we startd for the Columbia Mountain to winter with the Crow Indians who are our only friends in this country."

Because of Hugh's later connection with him, it is worth mentioning that tradition has made Étienne Provost — by some said not to have been an Ashley man at all — the leader of the group Potts was in. But whoever its chief may have been, he had received orders to try to find a usable pass through the mountains, too. Thus Ashley and Henry had independently decided that the only salvation of their company lay in reaching around the Blackfeet, and discovering a new beaver field in the Great Basin.

Because of Clyman's memoirs, much is known about Jed's party, while an eclipse of the news has made the movements of the other hard to follow. Logic says that its members rode along up the Big Horn to that stream's tributary, the Wind. Because of this, some historians have assumed that both bands of trappers wintered in the same Crow camp. Yet as neither Clyman nor Potts mentions a meeting which would seem guaranteed to have spurred comment from at least one of them, the guess has less than nothing to lean against. They must, rather, have holed up with separate divisions of the tribe which was their mutual host.

Newcomers to the mountains, Jed's party mistook a February thaw for the breaking of winter, and they nearly died of exposure, when a blizzard pounced, as they were trying to pierce the Tetons. Before the month was over, however, the weather softened enough on the Big Horn to let Hugh take up his chase again.

The nature of the message which Henry wished to send to Ashley has not been established, though probably it had to do with supplies, the location of his new station, and plans for the future which the Major then thought were original with him. At all events he wanted a dispatch taken to the lower Missouri, and in view of the travel conditions, as well as the Indians that might be met, Henry thought the messenger should have four companions.

Hall declared that Hugh himself was the messenger: "Finding that the trapper he was in pursuit of had gone to Fort Atkinson, Glass readily consented to be the bearer of letters for that post, and accordingly left Henry's Fort on the Big Horn River, on the 29th of February, 1824."

In writing to the same effect, Flagg pointed out that the mission was considered so dangerous that the Major once again dangled a premium as a lure for volunteers:

"At the time of the arrival of Glass at the Fort, some individiuals were sought for in the party by Major Henry, to take an express of great importance to Gen. Ashley, then at the Post of Council Bluffs, several hundred miles down the Missouri. Although a great reward had been offered, none of the company had expressed willingness to undertake a passage through a region infested by wandering hostile Indians at such an inclement season; but, no sooner was the enterprise proposed to Glass, than he, at once, acceeded to the terms, and . . . he started on the journey with four others, who volunteered to accompany him, by way of the Platte."

Ashley did not winter at Fort Atkinson; he was in St. Louis. The military post was, though, the nearest point which maintained regular communications with the metropolis on the Mississippi.

The names of the four men who went with Hugh were later given by the *St. Louis Enquirer* as Marsh, Chapman, More and Dutton. The latter was, of course, the man of that name whom the Reverend Orange Clark met in California and quizzed about Glass.

Because of the season they avoided the probably frozen Missouri and took a southerly route. Merely indicated by Flagg, it was described in detail by Hall: "They travelled across to Powder river which empties into the Yellow Stone, below the mouth of the Horn. They pursued their route up the Powder to its source, and thence across to the Platte. Here they constructed skin boats."

Being an old mountain man, Yount told Clark that what Hugh and his mates made was a "bullboat." Fashioned of buffalo hides stretched across withes, such a craft was normally as round as the sieve in which Edward Lear's Jumblies put to sea. If no doubt difficult to steer, it was the simplest of vessels to make, while its shallow draft made it suitable for the streams of scant water in the West.

Striking southeast from the headwaters of the Powder, Hugh and the others would have reached the North Platte in the vicinity of Casper, Wyoming. By the time their bullboat was built and its seams waterproofed by buffalo-bone glue, March must have pretty well run its course.

That the spring freshet, belonging to that time of the year, was at hand was explicit in Flagg's account. After bringing the trappers as far as the Platte, he wrote: "They had not proceeded far when a thaw came on — the ice of the stream broke up, and the adventurers were compelled as their only resource, to construct a skiff of Buffalo skins in order to continue on their route."

As Hugh had lived for years with the Wolf Pawnees, he was in, or was paddling toward, country with which he was familiar. What he didn't know was something which William Gordon, one of the pair who had set fire to the Ree villages, reported to the *National Intelligencer* of Washington a few months later: "These gentlemen [Keemly, another Missouri Fur Company man, as well as Gordon] also state, that about thirty lodges of Auricarees had gone across to the river Platte, and associated themselves with the Arapahoes and Chyans."

It was not just any band of Arikaras; it was the group which had broken with the rest of the tribe, when these had promised the Mandans peace with white men. The headless ghost of Grey Eyes was their gonfalon, and Elk's Tongue their Scanderbeg.

Glass and his fellows found this unbending crew where Laramie Creek joins the North Platte. A decade later this was to be the site of the famous Fort Laramie, but at the time none but Indian trails ran through the region. There are two explanations as to why the frontiersmen weren't wary. To understand Hall's version, it should be borne in mind that the Arikaras were allies of the Pawnees, who freely ranged in the hunting grounds of the latter tribe, and who spoke almost the same language:

"Here they constructed skin boats, and descended in them to the lower end of Les Cotes Noirs [the Black Hills] where they discovered thirty-eight lodges of Arickara Indians. This was the encampment of Gray-eyes' band. That chief had been killed in the attack of the American troops upon his village, and the tribe was now under the command of Langue de Biche [Elk's Tongue]. This warrior came down and invited our little party ashore, and, by many professions of friendship, induced them to believe him to be sincere. Glass had once resided with this *tonguey* old politician during a long winter, had joined him in the chase, and smoked his pipe, and cracked many a bottle by the genial fire of his wigwam. . . . The whites were thrown off their guard and accepted an invitation to smoke in the Indian's lodge."

With Yount concurring, though, Flagg asserted that because of the location of the band, and the similarity of the language to the one Hugh had spoken for years, he didn't at first grasp the fact that they were Rees: ". . . they proceeded several days, when they found themselves approaching a collection of Indian lodges standing upon the river bank, which they at once decided to be those of a friendly tribe of Pawnees. Paddling to the shore and landing, they left their rifles in the boat in charge of one of the company, and immediately advanced to the lodges in quest of provisions."

The one who remained with the bullboat was Dutton. The rest had hardly sat down with their hosts when, as Yount told Clark, Hugh heard a word or so pronounced in a way which caused him to warn his friends, "These are Pickarees."

To use Hall's phrasing, "the whites ran for life; the red warriors for blood." Cut off from their boat, the fugitives swam for it; though the opposite bank was as far as a couple of them got.

"Two of the party were overtaken and put to death: one of them within a few yards of Glass, who had gained a point of rocks unperceived and lay concealed from the view of his pursuers. Versed in all the arts of border warfare, our adventurer was able to practice them in the present crisis, with such success as to baffle his blood-thirsty enemies; and he remained in his lurking place until the search was abandoned in despair."

More and Chapman were the two whom Hugh had seen cut down. Dutton paddled the bullboat across the Platte, complete with a rifle, to aid him in escaping, as well as to take care of his needs when he got clear of the vicinity. Getting away in some undescribed manner, Marsh had the good luck to join forces with Dutton, so eating was not a problem for him, either. But Glass was once again forced to start making his way to a distant post, weaponless and alone.

Because of this second helping of one type of crisis, the episode has been hooted at by some who'd prefer not to believe in Hugh Glass; but the hooters have failed to take due notice of the St. Louis *Enquirer's* June 7,

1824, issue. An article in it quoted Louis Vasquez (an Ashley man who was later a fur trader himself, in partnership with Bill Sublette's younger brother, Andy):

Mr. Vasquez, just from the Upper Missouri, states that five men of Maj. Henry's party in descending the Platte, were attacked by a party of Aurikaree Indians — and that three, More, Chapman and Glass were killed; that the others, Dutton and Marsh, made their escape and arrived at Council Bluffs.

So as of some time in May, Marsh and Dutton succeeded in reaching Fort Atkinson, and there reported that the man who'd tangled with a grizzly bear, and lived, was now among the permanently missing. In the cases of the other two, the alarm was no false one — making his way down the Platte later that year, Clyman saw what was left of them, as well as the wreck of the bullboat; but Hugh's hourglass had plenty of sand left.

So did he; and its quality was that of jauntiness. By the standards of people who had not been left as he had been by Fitzgerald and Bridger, his predicament was desperate. Glass didn't think it so, according to a statement attributed to him by Hall:

"Although I had lost my rifle and all my plunder, I felt quite rich when I found my knife, flint and steel in my shot pouch. These little fixins make a man feel right peart when he is three or four hundred miles from anybody or any place."

His obvious course was to follow the Platte down, but, without a gun to aim at any further Arikaras who might be in the valley, he decided to cut away from the river and strike for Brazeau's trading post, instead of

Fort Atkinson. That meant traveling across country for the four hundred truly cited miles, with no sextant with which to shoot the sun. Yet Hugh was not now the tenderfoot who'd yawed from his desired line after having swum to the mainland from Campeachy. He made his point; and Hall declared that he lived well while on the way: "The buffaloe calves, at that season of the year, were generally but a few days old; and as the country through which he travelled was abundantly stocked with them, he found it no difficult task to overtake one as often as his appetite admonished him to."

He also made good, as Flagg pointed out, in his capacity as a courier: "The express to Gen. Ashley, which had been committed to his charge, he still bore, having preserved it safe from all his hardships."

But Hugh's own mission was still burning his mind. At Fort Kiowa he learned a bit of information which had probably been passed out by Black Harris, when he returned to the high Missouri as a free trapper, following a fling in St. Louis. John Fitzgerald had decided not to go back to beaver hunting. Instead, he had enlisted in the Sixth Regiment, which War Department records show that he did on April 19, 1824.

When Hugh took Henry's letter to Fort Atkinson, therefore, he demanded to see a certain member of the garrison. In Clark's manuscript such a meeting took place, ringing in a second preachy forgiveness scene, distinguished from the one with Bridger by its concluding injunction: "Give me my favorite Rifle!"

Floating tradition, and logic, however, back Hall's

contention that Hugh was balked of vengeance by the army's reluctance to have a soldier killed otherwise than in the line of duty:

"A journey of fifteen days brought him to Fort Kiawa. Thence he descended to Fort Atkinson, at the Council Bluffs, where he found his old traitorous acquaintance in the garb of a private soldier. This shielded the delinquent from chastisement. The commanding officer at the post ordered his rifle to be restored. . . ."

That restoration of property seems to have been arranged not by General Atkinson or Colonel Leavenworth but by the officer of the day. In this case it was said to have been Captain Bennet Riley, later a distinguished general and military governor of California. Always an efficient officer, he told the scarred trapper with the hot eyes that he couldn't have one of the post's soldiers to eat, but he saw to it that the frontiersman got his cherished weapon back with a minimum of delay.

So ended Hugh's quest in the service of love and hate; and the former proved stronger. While logging over two thousand miles, he mastered such an obstacle course as no one before had ever done, in order to get at the monster who'd stolen his star. But once he had his pet rifle in his hands again, he bore no one a grudge. Swearing Riley was a good fellow, he shook his hand and strode contentedly forth.

PART III

Afterclaps

6

/\/\/\/\/\/\

To the Southwest, and North Again

A man in this Countrey is not safe neither day nor night, and hardley ever expect to get back. this Countrey is the moste healthey in the world I believe.
— LETTER BY DANIEL T. POTTS

THE NARRATIVE of James Hall carries Hugh no farther than the regaining of his rifle, in May or June of 1824, at Fort Atkinson. With Cooke already silent, only two of the four main accounts say what befell Glass after the achievement of his central adventure.

Clark was told by Yount that the fame of Hugh's mishaps and exploits induced the Sixth Regiment to pass the hat for a man wronged by one of their new recruits: "At the Fort a purse of Three Hundred Dollars was bestowed upon him and with this money he travelled to the extremely western settlements on the Missouri and became a partner in an enterprise of trading in New Mexico."

He was presumably, too, capitalized by the message-to-Garcia reward paid him by Henry. But at all events, Flagg agreed that Hugh joined merchants bound for the sunset side of the southern Plains: "One would suppose, that the hardships undergone by Glass would have effectually taken from him all desire, ever again to try his fortunes in the wilderness. But it was not so. . . . A trading party was formed to go to Santa Fe, and with it went Glass."

One reason why he temporarily separated himself from the fur trade was the bad news from that industry, as practiced on the Upper Missouri. The white scalps lost bid fair to outnumber the beaver pelts gained. Ashley's plan to bring trappers up the river had thus far been an unproductive experiment, costly in blood as well as dollars. Cayewa Brazeau's try to deal with the Mandans and Rees hadn't worked out for his French syndicate. Tilton had finally had to abandon his Columbia Fur Company post and take refuge with the Mandans. Pilcher's Missouri Fur Company was coasting toward the bankruptcy which soon bunkered it.

Along the Santa Fe Trail, though, things looked promising for men who didn't mind having to dodge past scalping knives on the way to their sales outlets. Pawnee, Kiowa, Comanche and Apache war parties were standard hazards, while Crows, Arikaras and Gros Ventres might also swoop that far south. But the trail served a market which funneled goods of American manufacture throughout northern Mexico, via the distributing point of Chihuahua City. And through the same great mart, a people hungry for the products of the Industrial Age exchanged silverware, fine leatherwork, embroidered textiles and furs for tinware and other cheaply made goods of mass manufacture.

Up to 1824, those who had followed William Becknell to Santa Fe had burdened pack mules, but in that year merchants began loading wagons with the stuff of trade with Mexico. From Independence, Missouri, the canvas-topped vans with the huge wheels creaked and swayed for eight hundred miles before making port in the plaza of an isolated capital.

Indians weren't the only wayside hazard. Then as now Kansas was high-wind country; and the sun which sucked water holes dry was another enemy.

Even when the merchant caravans had rolled around the toe of the Rockies and reached north and west into the long-settled valley of the Rio Grande, they were not safe. In the fall of 1824, for example, Comanches burned ranches, stole stock, slew men and kidnaped women on the outskirts of Santa Fe itself.

Yet Americans did not only ply back and forth on a do-or-die trail, they stayed where two-and-a-half centuries of civilization had made so little headway against barbarity. Most that did so remained because of the fur trade, which was there offering the rewards for risk, which the industry was failing to provide on the Upper Missouri.

Among those who drove mules as far as Santa Fe — and let whoever cared to urge them back to the States — were such former Ashley men as Tom (later to be known as Peg-leg) Smith and the Jim Kirker whom the Apaches rechristened Santiago. A third Ashley Alumnus, coming to trade but remaining to trap, was Hugh Glass.

Perhaps the many weeks of riding behind, or keeping

pace with, slowly plodding mules had convinced him that a Western merchant's life was not for him. But if he hadn't made up his mind by the time he arrived in New Mexico, he speedily returned to a less confining way of life upon learning how other trappers were faring in the Southwest. "On arriving there," to quote Flagg, "he joined a trapping expedition to the river Helo, a small stream said to empty into the Gulf of California."

In pre-irrigation days, the Gila was seasonally a good-sized stream, which joined the Colorado before blending its waters with the gulf in question. A river that threaded hundreds of miles of desert between thin stands of verdure, the Gila's source lay in mountains framing the valley of the Rio Bravo del Norte, as local Mexicans styled the upper Rio Grande.

Probably Hugh trapped only its New Mexico headwaters, in 1824, as there is no report of Americans venturing into Arizona until a year or so later. Aside from such westerly expeditions, and a few which fared south along the streams of Sonora, the exiles began to look northward for beaver, from the opening of 1825 on.

Taos, rather than Santa Fe, was their headquarters; and that's where Yount said that Hugh went at about this time. Seventy miles north and east of the capital, the little mountain community was frequented by as notable a gathering of beaver skinners as ever pitched whiskey past their beards. Ewing Young was of their number; so were James Ohio Pattie, Bill Sublette's brother Milton, Tom timber-peg Smith, Old Bill Williams, and Santiago Kirker. All had great stories; but as this is that of Hugh Glass, it is fitting to remark that George Yount was one of the man-size adventurers who worked, fought and frolicked beside the epic figures.

Sifted for furs by so many men of extraordinary skill and energy, the streams of an arid region were not productive for any great while. The men of Taos were, on this account, forced to range ever farther north, before returning to dispose of their peltries and buy easy women and hard liquor with their gains.

In the main they veered west of north, thus avoiding the battalion of towering peaks in Colorado, which was the last area in that time belt to be frisked by trappers. Instead they rode along the rivers of Utah — the San Juan, the Colorado, the Price, the Escalante, the Muddy, the Grand, the Green — and so up the Great Basin toward tributaries of the northwesterly winding Snake. Beside that branch of the Columbia, or one of its feeders, Hugh was put to another endurance test. Yount and Flagg describe it in much the same fashion; but before their versions are compared, note must be taken of the fact that Yount prefaced his by telling Clark that Glass was hired "to conduct a band of trappers into the territory of the Eutaws" by Étienne Provost.

This is the same individual whom chroniclers, and ones with the best of credentials, believe to have been the leader of a party sent into the Crow country in the fall of 1823. Assuming that is correct, an explanation of why he moved from the edge of the Tetons, to a point much farther from great trapping country, belongs in this narrative. Then, as connecting circumstances are keys to an understanding of Hugh's later moves, they will also be given here, before the events they refer to lag too far back for easy remembering.

While Glass, Dutton *et al.* had been making their way from Fort Henry to their meeting with Rees at the future site of Fort Laramie, two non-co-operating parties of the Rocky Mountain Fur Company were skirting the Rockies looking for a pass through the mountains blocked by neither too much snow nor warring redskins.

Andrew Henry's luck stayed by him as never did familiar by a witch. After long searching, of which the details are vague, the men he had sent crossed the mountains only to find themselves little better off than they had been when east of the Rockies. At last discouraged by their report, this first cousin of Job decided to give up the fur trade. According to a newspaper report dated August 30, 1824, he was then in St. Louis. Not having heard from the men whom he himself had dispatched west, Ashley was ready to forget beaver as a source of fortune, too; and the partnership was dissolved.

At this very time Tom Fitzpatrick was racing starvation down the Platte, a message for General Ashley his only freight except a bulletless rifle. The message was from Jed Smith, patroon of the party which Ashley had launched from Fort Kiowa the previous September.

Ed Rose — to get him out of a story in which he didn't figure — had repaired his political fences by giving away Ashley's trade goods, and was enjoying the status of a Crow chief again, when Smith made his try to pierce the mountains in February. Having learned about mountain blizzards in the Wind River zone, Jed turned his back to the North Pole. Not long afterward, he and his companions began tracing the Sweetwater to its source, at the east end of the doorway through the Rockies known as South Pass.

They encountered no Blackfeet, or any other posters of No TRESPASSING signs, as they proceeded across the divide to the headwaters of the Sandy, and down that stream to the Green. There were beaver lagoons all along this river, and, behind dams built at all suitable points along numerous tributaries, humped clusters of their water-surrounded lodges.

The white men had some trouble with the resident Shoshones over horses, because they were Indians and always stole horses; but the Snakes didn't try to stop Smith's party from taking beaver, which, here, no fur trading company had taught them to prize.

Neither did the beaver put difficulties in the trappers' way. Unschooled to wariness, they raced each other to be the first to be caught in sunken traps, baited with an essence brewed from the dog genitals of their own kind.

So the upshot, as warm weather closed the trapping season by cheapening animal coats, was a take of many more pelts than the mustangs on hand could carry away. The surplus cached, or stored in pits sealed against rainfall and burrowing beasts, the rest went up to South Pass a-horseback.

At this point Smith decided to return to the Great Basin and chart more beaver waters. Needing all the pack animals for his new undertaking, he had none to spare the men charged with bearing good news — and a certain amount of furs — eastward. Jed therefore relied on the Sweetwater to be more navigable than it was.

Already plumbing the possibilities of that river, Jim Clyman was chased by a war party of some unguessed nation. In consequence, he was scored as lost, while he in turn deemed himself the party's surviving solitaire. He then commenced the long walk to Fort Atkinson (milestoned at one point by the discovery of Hugh's bullboat, and two of its once alive crew).

Smith, Bill Sublette and six others had by this time turned back to what was then all known as Oregon. In due course Fitzpatrick, not yet with missing fingers, built another bullboat, with the help of the two men left with him. None of them knew whither the Sweetwater flowed, but they hoped it might unite with the Platte. That turned out to be correct. They also trusted that the river would have no staircases to fall down. The Sweetwater was not that sweet, however: at one point it was vertical instead of horizontal, and after a brief flight through the air, the boat floated again, but downside up.

Dived for, the pelts were dried and cached. A gun or so was also salvaged. But, as little powder was again usable if rescued at all, it was a pinched threesome who arrived at Fort Atkinson in mid-September.

Clyman was already there, but as he had no certain knowledge as to how the rest had fared, he had sent no word to St. Louis. Fitzpatrick, though, had Jed Smith's letter to Ashley; and he knew of two fur caches along the Sweetwater, in addition to the one on the Green. So the next boat which carried dispatches south from Fort Atkinson took with it the word that the dying Western fur trade had a chance to flourish as never before.

The promise sped up the Missouri as well as down. It brought no hope to the river-shackled companies, for they were geared only to deal for pelts brought into their posts. But it mightily cheered other Ashley men. For they had been adrift, after Major Henry had decided to go back to mining, or whatever he did, following his return to St. Louis.

In spite of the fact that their prospects weren't shiny, most of the former garrison of Fort Henry decided to carry on with trap and gun. This was hardly strange in view of the alternative which menaced most of these young fellows. Back in the States, they and their mules would have been hitched to plows furrowing somebody else's acres.

Jim Bridger was one who preferred riding an animal to working in harness with it; but he and the rest who made this choice were at first no better than wilderness hangers-on. Unlike the men of Taos, they had no ready market. Nor did they have any but picked-over hunting grounds, until they got the tidings which sent them over South Pass, there to bloom as that transient triumph of the wilds: the beaver-rich mountain men.

Yet the newspaper articles citing Andrew Henry's retreat to St. Louis mention that a number of his men were with him. Étienne Provost would have logically been one of these, because he was a man of commercial enterprise, who wouldn't have stayed with hard scrabble in the name of independence only.

So he was probably on hand when Jed Smith's relayed letter arrived, and Ashley began readying to cash in on the desperation dice he had thrown at Fort Kiowa. But, aside from the unexplained tradition that Ashley and Provost had quarreled, the General wasn't inviting partners. His good luck, and Henry's bad, had given the General first whack at a mother lode of peltries. He'd taken his lumps alone, and now he would whistle that way.

Frozen out of the American West, Provost raised the capital to set himself up as a trader in New Mexico, where, historically, he was established by the spring of 1825. By the time he reached Taos, besides, he had thought of a way to get a cut of Ashley's melon.

What had seemed the weak point of the General's position was the distance separating scattered teams of trappers from a market linked to them by no river highway. But Ashley's genius beat the problem. Packing whiskey and lesser trade goods up the Platte and over the mountains, he established the open-air fur mart, known as a "rendezvous," when 1825 grew mild.

Until the success of that maneuver was evident, Provost had probably hoped to be able to channel much, if not most, of the mountain beaver trade through Taos, which was a much closer market than any in Missouri. As it was, though, the best he could do was to send out trappers, under contract to hunt in the rich northern fields and bring the pelts back to his station.

There is thus no reason to doubt Yount's statement that Hugh arranged, with Provost, to lead a trapping party which wound up in faraway Shoshone country. Flagg added the detail that a man named DuBreuil was of the company.

At the given seven hundred miles away from Taos, Hugh and his trappers must have been on the Snake itself, and well west toward Oregon, on an uncalled day in 1825, or possibly the following year. In either case they were trapping with the convenience of a canoe. Covering their line in this craft, they had pulled into it several animals, promptly skinned by one of those not wielding a paddle.

Caught beaver were normally eaten as well as flayed, and the tail was valued as a delicacy. But Yount said that, on this occasion, Hugh's party had a surplus they were moved to give away, when they saw a solitary Indian woman seated on the bank. Her back was turned, but, secure in their charitable intentions, they didn't bother to cough or clear their throats. She on her part was perhaps deaf or dozing, for she didn't look their way, when the white men beached their canoe.

Still without drawing her notice, Hugh and some others each hoisted a beaver carcase. It wasn't until they were within a few feet of her that she saw them and rewarded their thoughtfulness with a shriek which drew male Shoshones.

So much for Yount's account, as interpreted, and possibly bowdlerized, by the Reverend Orange Clark. The wording of Flagg's version uprears no such picture of disinterested benevolence:

"At length, early one morning, as they were ascending the river, they perceived a squaw upon the eastern bank digging for roots. They immediately ran their *pirogue* silently along beneath the shore until they arrived opposite the woman, when they landed and advanced toward her, holding out a beaver which they had caught the night before as a peace-offering."

But Flagg agrees with Clark's manuscript as to how she reacted:

"The instant, that she saw them, she raised a frightful yell, and from the neighboring bushes rushed out a powerful Indian with a bow and arrows in his hands. It was in vain that the hunters signified to him their peaceful purposes. He placed an arrow on his bowstring and raised it to his eye to launch the shaft, when Glass and his companion turned and ran with all speed for their rifles, which they had left in the skiff. Before reaching it, two or three arrows from the savage had wounded Glass in the back, and just as DuBreuil was raising his rifle to fire, an arrow passed through his throat and he fell dead at the same moment with the Indian!"

Yount's version is much more circumstantial. According to him, Hugh didn't repeat the mistake of leaving his gun behind when stepping ashore. He told Clark, too, that quite a number of braves rose out of screened resting-places in answer to the squaw's scream.

The volley of arrows they launched mortally wounded one of the trappers — in all likelihood DuBreuil, though given no name. He killed an Indian, after being brought down, but he wanted to see another dust-biter before he closed his eyes for keeps.

Ahead of him in flight, Hugh hadn't been hit. He had, moreover, a good chance of reaching the canoe unscathed, until he undertook to answer the prayer of DuBreuil, or his double. Unable to reload his rifle, the dying man begged not to be left without a shot to fire at the Indians closing in to finish him.

Dashing back, Hugh charged the gun. Urged to do so by a man who knew himself done for, Glass then resumed flight; but when he turned his back to archers this second time, one of them scored.

The men already at the canoe were able to report that the one Hugh had stopped to arm had made use of his last strength to squeeze a baneful trigger. In the ring and not a spectator, Glass the while was running, as fast as can be expected of a man who has a chunk of metal imbedded in one of the bones of his spine.

Tugging didn't dislodge it, and its location made the other trappers leery of trying any other means of extraction. So Hugh carried the arrowhead. He carried it in his spine while riding seven hundred miles over un-curried country.

Flagg was no doubt wrong in ascribing the use of poisoned arrows. Unlike the Modocs, the Snakes weren't noted for this variety of chemical warfare. But Flagg and Yount both were safe this side of guesswork, when they agreed that the wound festered. And that type of poison had many a day in which to feed upon itself and grow mighty.

Such was the surgical case that Hugh Glass brought to doctorless Taos, but there was a chap present who wasn't feazed by it. After giving Hugh the standard beaker of whiskey and a bullet to bite, a man, unlikely to have heard of sterilization, cut the arrowhead free of pus and bone with his tool for shaving.

In Western annals, this medical feat ranks second to none — not even the celebrated removal of iron from the back of Jim Bridger. For Dr. Marcus Whitman, who carved on that latter occasion (while mountain men goggled and Indians jabbered in half the tongues of the land), had a professional's kit of instruments. Yet the owner of the cool hand which snicked death from Hugh's spine is not known, because the chronicler who had the one shot at this episode didn't pass on what he was, unquestionably, told.

"Yount," wrote Orange Clark, "well knew the hardy trapper who performed this awful operation with a razor." But the reverend fathead earned consignment to where ministers aren't supposed to go, by a monstrous sin of omission. He failed to give a now dead hero his earned niche in recollection.

Because of this shadowy figure's nerve and skill, Glass not only survived but was restored to campaign vigor. "Sooner than could have been expected," to employ Flagg's understatement, "he recovered from his injuries, and the next we hear of him he is hunting and trapping, with *one* companion as usual, at the headwaters of the Missouri. . . ."

Hugh wound up back on the high Missouri, albeit not so soon as Flagg implied. First he was drawn away from Taos by a combination of fur trade developments and his own bents.

The annual rendezvous remained a fixture, even when Ashley retired, his hairy fortune made in a couple of years. For a fat consideration, he passed the beaver baton to Jed Smith, who took as partners Bill Sublette and David Jackson. Although Bill came to be one of the storied mountain men, the other was a mysterious figure. He was of the inner circle of the great wilderness adventurers, but the only plume history stuck in his medicine hat was the discovery of the vale east of the Tetons, still known as Jackson's Hole.

The remarkable thing about this trio of merchants was that they had neither home office nor outpost trading stations. Ashley had operated out of St. Louis. The firm of Smith, Jackson and Sublette bought trade goods in Missouri and disposed of furs there, but their place of business was mountain country, unlimited. Their storage warehouses and supply depots were caches, guarded from robbers only by the cleverness with which they were made to look as though no one had ever dug there. Their stock stables and corrals were buckskin hobbles, to keep mounts and pack animals from ranging so far that they couldn't be caught again. Their conference rooms were buffalo robes spread beside a spring or campfire. Their only address was wherever the rendezvous might be held in any given year.

For all its wildness, and it was an unpoliced orgy in one of its many phases, the rendezvous was an efficient business institution. Its greatest single accomplishment was to keep expert trappers where the beaver were the year round. Had it not been for the annual bazaar, with all its side attractions, a bunch of shagbarks, of an age to have their sap running free, would have often sought the release of spring blowouts in the States. Figuring in travel time, east and west, months would have been periodically shucked from the hunting schedule of every prosperous young elk, newly in horn.

But with the rendezvous to look forward to, the trappers held their steam valve down, and brought a full count of pelts to market. Celibacy didn't menace them, for squaws could be leased, bought, secured on loan or won at gambling. The blood call of a spree could have drawn them, nevertheless, to where they might have been tempted to linger with women of their own kind. The rendezvous stood between them and the pull of the settlements; and they became wedded to the vast and sparsely peopled community of which it was the focal point.

The place and date of the next such meeting was set at the last. When the time drew near, the few hundred mountain men began converging from separate points in their realm of over a half million square miles. If they weren't killed en route, they brought their beaver bullion to exchanges, where the tepees of several brands of Indians outnumbered the bivouacs of frontiersmen.

The bargaining was gauged by the grades of the pelts, which had to be established by marketplace examination. His buying power thus arranged and chalked up, the mountain man asked for powder, shot and caps enough to see him through another year; he asked for field equipment, simple as a cup or complex as a telescope; he asked for the fanciest shirt and best slouch hat on display; he asked for gaudy bolts of cloth and costume jewelry, on behalf of any squaw that might be in or near his life; he asked for tobacco and whiskey — and there he had the substance of what he thought to buy with a year of hazardous toil.

Potts told what it was often like, and what their hardihood was cheerfully balanced against: "Here I got straid away from my company and fell in with Indians who were not Crows and traveld thirty miles from one hour by sun in the evening until midnight accross the mountains through Snow up to my middle wich frose my feet severely so that I lost two toes etire and two others in part from this I didn't recover until late in the spring nevertheless I made this spring with the addition of ten days last fall three hundred and fifty Dollars and the ensewing fall and spring I expect to make about twelve hundred Dollars if nothing happens more than I know of."

Yet rendezvous days, of which there were enough to make weeks, were halcyon days. When a man had finished trading, he was free to watch or take part in horse races, foot races, shooting matches, wrestling bouts, card games and Indian gambling with sticks. There was horse trading, knife swapping, lie swapping; and there would have been squaw chasing, if the squaws hadn't met enthusiasts more than halfway. There was shoptalk about guns, furs, streams and regional conditions. There was misty loafing with John Barleycorn and other good friends, on the part of men whose normal days consisted of harsh struggle and peering for enemies.

The talk then could and did sound the unfolding geography of their private empire. Jim Bridger had gone down Bear River and found a mass of salt water which was linked with no ocean. Jed Smith had gone west across a desert to Mexican California, and on the way back he had pierced a range as tall as the Rockies. And Bill Sublette led a party which had found something more marvelous than both of the other troves combined. Potts was with him, and he wrote of it to a relative he addressed as "Respectid Brother":

". . . the Luchkadee or Calliforn Stinking fork Yellow-stone South fork or Masuri and Henrys fork all those head at an angular point that of the Yellow-stone had a large fresh water lake near its head on the verry top of the Mountain which is about one hundrid by fourty miles in diameter and as clear as crystal on the south borders of this lake is a number of hot and boiling springs some of water and others of most beautiful fine clay and resembles that of a mush pot and throws its particles to the immense height of from twenty to thirty feet in height The clay is white and of a pink and water appears fathomless as it appears to be entirely hollow under neath. There is also a number of places where the pure suphor is sent forth in abundance one of our men Visited one of those wilst taking his recreation there at an instan the earth began a tremendious trembling and he with difficulty made his escape when an explosion took place resembling that of thunder."

The talk ranged over battles involving trappers and tribesmen. One such fight enlivened the Bear Lake rendezvous of 1827, at which Glass was present. Although showing up too late to be an eyewitness, Potts left an account, warm with the breath of the spectator he had just talked to:

"A few Days previous to my arrival at this place a party of about 120 Black feet approachid the Camp and killed a Snake and his squaw the alarm was immediately given and the Snakes Utaws and Whites sallied forth for battle the enemy fled to the Mountain to a small concavity thickly groon with small timber surrounded by open ground In this engagement the squaws where busily engaged in throwing up batterys an draging off the dead there was only six whites engaged in this battle who immediately advanced within pistol shot and you may be assured that every shot counted one the loss of the Snakes was three killed and the same wounded that of the Whites one wounded and two narrowly made their escape that of the Utaws was none though who gained great applause for their bravery the loss of the enemy is not known six where found dead on the ground besides a great number where carried off on Horses."

The talk covered individual exploits. They told of how Bill Sublette and Black Harris had snowshoed out of the Rockies on rendezvous business. They spoke of how Johnson Gardner had wrecked the hopes of a horning-in Hudson's Bay Company brigade. They spoke of how Peg-leg Smith began cutting off his natural left leg, when its splintering by a bullet threatened him with gangrene. More than all others, they spoke of Hugh Glass, whom they all knew by sight as well as repute.

There is nothing to show just when Hugh ceased to trap out of Taos, but Flagg implies that he took to living completely in the wilds as soon as his spine was in sound working order once more. Probably, in that case, it was at some point during 1826 that he shucked his last ties with anything approaching settlement.

The severance wound up an evolution right down the alley of Darwin. After his capture first by pirates and then by Pawnees, Hugh had won to St. Louis. Already with the rating of one of America's principal cities, that river port could not have been found jarringly different, when matched against the ones which he had known as a salt in the sense of mariner. By his own choice, though, Glass had left all marches of civilization for points westward.

While with Lafitte and the Pawnees, he had chewed a distinct soul's cud of silence, whether or not that had before been his lot. Up the Missouri he had been of a company only until Old Ephraim had made him as solitary as a star without planets. He had tried the com-

merce of the Santa Fe Trail and found its returns worth
less than a chance to wander at large. For a time he had
kept one toe in settled New Mexico; but the sensualities
of that Spanish woods colt lacked the appeal they held
for many younger American frontiersmen.

Or perhaps it would be more accurate to forget his
years and lean wholly on the fact that he had learned
self-sufficiency under circumstances which make Robinson Crusoe seem like a pampered whelp of decadence.
Glass had developed certain extraordinary talents, in
sum, and because wild country was where they were at
home, the mountain man's kingdom of singletons was
his natural locus.

Yount made it plain that Hugh astonished even a
crew of ferociously independent scatterlings by his
scorn of group co-operation. When first met by fellow
Westerners, as has earlier been stated, he was given to
prowling apart from his companions when on the
march. By the time Yount had made his acquaintance,
he had enlarged his autonomy by sleeping of nights by
his separate campfire. The others often didn't know
where this was located, as Clark was furthermore told;
but Hugh always knew where the others were, and answered any shout of alarm by swiftly rallying.

So he grew to be a wilderness celebrity, for more reasons than his craft and courage in postponing death.
His preferred loneliness awed, if it at times annoyed,
less monolithic characters. Then, his preserved letter
shows him to have been possessed of a quaint dignity
of mind, which put him beyond the understanding of

the much younger and jauntier wights, who commonly took cleansing hangovers away from this or that rendezvous.

They trusted Hugh, though. That was not only declared by Yount; it was demonstrated by what transpired at one of the turning points of the fur trade.

For four years after Tom Fitzpatrick was handed a letter for Ashley by Jed Smith, its history had been primarily that of the roving mountain man. The old forts along the Missouri did little business, or were abandoned; and where trade goods had once been universally borne up the river in keel or Mackinaw boats, the main market was now supplied by overland pack trains.

The small Missouri companies vainly tried to wedge into the monopoly, which Ashley had passed on to the Rocky Mountain Fur Company of Smith, Jackson and Sublette. But the newcomers couldn't compete, in the field, with the primary mountain men, nor did they have the capital to establish a diversionary market.

This last, however, was in the wallets of the American Fur Company, financed by John Jacob Astor and other Eastern men of substance. Usually not named, it will be revealed here that the substance was greenbacks. They had been acquired in various ways, including Amfurco operations in other regions. By 1828, though, the American Fur Company had decided to revive the high Missouri market, and to crash that of the mountains. To this end its moguls established a special Western Division, and hired a Scotch import, called

Kenneth McKenzie, to bring all bacon in sight home to Wall Street.

McKenzie was a gifted piranha who could seem a goldfish when it served his purpose. While eager for any barbarity which would gain his point, he wouldn't balk at decent methods if they proved to be the only trumps.

Elsewhere the American Fur Company, like that of Hudson's Bay, had secured furs in one of two fashions. Its factors had either bought whatever pelts Indians might bring into trading stations, or they had sent out brigades of hired half-breed trappers. As ill-paid as the redskins, if possible, these were shackled in serfdom by being allowed to spend a smidgen more than their pittances each year.

The American free trapper posed a different problem. He knew, as Indians did not, the dollar value of various grades of pelts. He also knew the worths of trade items, and he wasn't going to swap a beaver plew for the two-for-a-nickle gimcracks fobbed off on savages.

Seeing that, McKenzie set generosity as the policy where mountain men were concerned. He had to have them, to crack the high country market, so he put it on the grapevine that the Western Division of the American Fur Company was paying higher prices than had ever been heard of, for prime pelts. That meant mountain pelts, for the beaver in lower and prevailingly warmer regions grew inferior coats.

Prior to 1828, his organization had had no station

within feasible delivery range for mountain men, but when McKenzie gave the winds his price bulletin, he was bringing upriver the wherewithal to build a post, to be located on the north bank of the Missouri, four miles west of the mouth of the Yellowstone. Arrived, he began laying the foundations of what was originally called Fort Floyd.

Where most of the mountain men first heard of McKenzie's artful honesty was the rendezvous of 1828. Like that of the year before, it was held at Bear Lake — sometimes called Sweet Lake, to distinguish it from the neighboring salty one found by Jim Bridger.

McKenzie's messenger was Étienne Provost, who had joined the American Fur Company upon discovering that he couldn't get much of the beaver trade by operating in Taos. What Étienne hoped to accomplish was to lure a great many top-notch trappers to Fort Floyd by waving McKenzie's glittering scale of prices.

His proposition undercut the structure of the fur trade as set up by General Ashley. If it didn't promptly cause the free trappers to ditch the market central to their way of life, it led them to look at their situation with sharper eyes.

When they did so, they could not be as pleased with the firm of Smith, Jackson and Sublette as they had been. They now saw themselves as the tools of a monopoly.

Aiming to establish one himself, McKenzie knew the physique of such a business clear down to the heel which Achilles also owned. This was identical with its source of strength: a monopoly was a Hobson's choice dictatorship, which it was second nature to resent, once the question of the abuse of privilege was ever raised.

For men with the talents to acquire one, the instinct to take advantage of a monopoly has rarely proved more controllable than St. Vitus's dance. Granted the sole keep of a generally needed or coveted item, the purveyors end by screwing the price turns beyond the level of fairness.

Knowing that much, on the basis of human percentage, McKenzie probably knew more, based on what he had been able to learn of the merchants he was trying to break. There are no grounds for suspecting that any of them had other than hard-bargain yearnings. A passionate explorer with an itch for religion, Jed Smith had taught the Hudson's Bay Company that he was no one to whom anybody who prized them should expose his eyeteeth. Another great outdoorsman, Bill Sublette eventually nailed himself behind office walls, where he didn't want to be, through his dollar-grabbing bent. Although no footnoted characteristic can be assigned to David Jackson, logic says that a tough business head topped his shadowy figure, or he wouldn't have been welcomed as a partner by the other two.

But Smith, Jackson and Sublette didn't have to be prodigies of greed, once Étienne Provost started explaining how little they were giving for furs as compared with what could be gained at Fort Floyd. McKenzie's maneuver was designed to make everybody forget the markups to which merchants who put wares beyond the Rockies were entitled; and the take-it-or-leave-it position of the men who ran the fresh-air bazaars did the rest.

The one thing on the side of the Rocky Mountain Fur Company was that the enamored trappers didn't want to leave the Rocky Mountains. Nor did they wish to forfeit the rendezvous as a social as well as a commercial institution.

The result was that they took their jugs to a convention, at which it was decided to offer the Western Division of the American Fur Company a counter-proposition. McKenzie himself wrote that the man the free trappers chose as their delegate was Hugh Glass.

Typically, he carried out the assignment alone. From Bear Lake he went east over the Rockies to the headwaters of the Big Horn. At the highest point navigable for such a craft, he fashioned a bullboat and took to the water. Cruising down the river, he passed the mouth of the Little Big Horn, and then what was left of the post where he had found and forgiven young Bridger. On the Yellowstone, next, he sped toward the stretch of the Missouri which he had crossed on a pair of logs, following his snow-beset walk from Mandanland. Westing, against the current, he paddled by the fort where he had expected to slay both Jim and Fitzgerald, and arrived at the one which McKenzie meant to make the headquarters of the entire Western fur trade.

7

∧∧∧∧∧∧

With His Moccasins On

A man of the name of Gardner, who afterwards
happened to meet with these Indians, killed two of
them with his own hand, and I received the scalp of
one of them, as a present during my stay in the fort.
— PRINCE MAXIMILIAN OF WIED

THE NAME of Fort Floyd was changed to Fort
Union following the abandonment of a post, situ-
ated two hundred miles farther up the Missouri, which
had borne that name. When completed, the Amfurco
station was as relatively imposing as McKenzie had intended it to be. Twenty feet tall, palings hewn from tree-
trunks walked around an area two hundred and forty
feet long by two hundred in width. The southwest and
northeast corners were guarded by stone bastions,
twenty-four feet square and thirty high. The lower
stories of these were pierced for cannon. The big guns
could be used to police the plaza, as well as to keep
hostiles at a distance. This was a needful flexibility, because the Indians, whose co-operation McKenzie bought
with firewater, occasionally ran amok.

When trouble of that nature was foreseen in time, according to the memoirs of an American Fur Company hand named Larpenteur, a tranquilizing cocktail was made by lacing the hooch with laudanum. The whiskey in turn was the dubious product of the still Fort Union wasn't supposed to have. McKenzie paid Indians to hijack the furs of other firms. McKenzie would rob, ruin or rub out anybody not on his team. He was a one-man crime wave; but he had charm, and people he wished to like him generally did so.

He knew how to deal with Hugh Glass, when the latter reached Fort Union in the fall of 1828. Here was a man whose co-operation the trader very much wanted; and he listened as well as talked.

What Hugh had been authorized to do on behalf of his fellow free trappers was to invite McKenzie to send trade goods to the next rendezvous, thereby breaking the Rocky Mountain Fur Company's monopoly. While the Amfurco chieftain would have willingly complied, he couldn't — for two reasons.

In the first place, he didn't yet have the trained personnel. Taking a packtrain through the Rockies, in time to trade at a rendezvous, was a business for experts who knew where, and how soon, grass would be high enough to support hungry animals at all points along the way. Only long-term mountain men could boast that knowledge — or had minds which were maps of the region's watering points, and trails safe for laden animals under all conditions.

Secondly, McKenzie was handicapped by his very determination to make his headquarters the master key of the fur trade. Even granting him skilled packtrain leaders, he knew he couldn't — or couldn't until steamers began chugging up the high Missouri several years later — get a fresh supply of trade goods up the river in keelboats, early enough to compete with those who brought them overland along the Platte.

After discussing such problems with Hugh, the trader came back to his original proposition, though sweetened to the taste of free trappers. He asked Glass to tell his fellows that they could operate anywhere and in any fashion they chose to, and that, in return for their signing contracts to bring their furs to Fort Union, the American Fur Company would guarantee better than fair prices. Agreed upon in writing, in advance of delivery, these would be redeemable in cash.

It was a good offer, with but one drawback. It linked any takers to a specific point on the map, and one with permanent buildings on it. That cut at mountain-man pride — for one of their boasts had come to be that there were no strings which bound them to anything resembling the channeled ways of life which they had left behind in the States.

How many were tempted by McKenzie's bait, after Glass reported to his constituents at the rendezvous of 1829, there is nothing to indicate. Yet a development of 1830 made Hugh choose a fur-trade formula which left him a better-heeled free agent.

It had to do with Jim Bridger. Rebounding from the shock of finding Glass alive, as tradition has believably sworn, Jim matured with the suddenness of apples visited by frost. This is borne out by history's testimony, for within a couple of years he had become a brigade leader with a mother grouse's grave view of responsibilities. When older and more assured, he relaxed and learned to laugh again; but his earnestness while he was still trying to prove himself caused fellow trappers to dub a still very young man "Old Gabe."

They said it affectionately, though. Bridger was liked for his decency, and admired for his deeds as an explorer and Indian fighter.

Mountain-man cream, Jim was one of those logically in line to take over the rendezvous when Smith, Jackson and Sublette decided to sell their firm. The buyers had to be wilderness mandarins, for the prestige of its directing paladins was the only cement which held together the parts of the world's most remarkable commercial enterprise.

Still five years short of being known by his hardwon nickname of Broken Hand, Tom Fitzpatrick was the signal caller of the newest and last Rocky Mountain Fur Company — which was the only one to be publicly so known. As associates, he took, in chief, three. He chose Milton Sublette, whom some songbird of the fourth estate had once tabbed as "the Thunderbolt of the Rockies"; he chose Henry Fraeb, later considered by an experienced witness the ugliest corpse a bullet had ever put on display; and he chose Old Gabe Bridger.

As of 1830, in short, Jim had become one of the high rollers of the mountain fur trade. He was one of those who set up the rendezvous layout, issued the chips, called their values, dealt the cards, and raked in the profits. Such were the benefits of being an officer of the new monopoly; but they were probably begrudged

Bridger by a man who remembered what it was like to be an invalid left naked of equipment in wilds traversed by war parties.

This is theory, with only reasoning for legs. There is not the slightest saved hint as to how the two reacted to the fact that they were jointly present at several rendezvous. Yet perhaps that silence stands for description enough. They were two good men, but, because of what had taken place, they could not in decency associate. They knew what they knew; and there was no bridge across the chasm but that of a false heartiness foreign to both.

That is not to postulate a feud, pensioned by brooding to outlast all occasion for it. But with an alternative up his sleeve, there is no reason why Glass should have wished to do business with, and add to the prosperity of, a firm owned in part by a man he'd rather not think about.

So on that ground, as it would seem just to believe, he seceded from the main body of mountain men, most of whom continued to meet at a time and place set by the Rocky Mountain Fur Company. Thereafter, Glass appears to have justified Flagg's insistence that he took only such beaver as were to be found east of the Great Divide.

That summarizes all that either Flagg or Yount had to say of the semifinal phase of Hugh's existence. Chittenden, though, was able to add one detail, gathered when he was on the high Missouri half a century later. South across the river from the site of Fort Union rose highlands which old-timers still called Glass's Bluffs, because of the tradition that Hugh used to hunt bighorn sheep there.

More would be known if a certain manuscript, written by an inmate of Fort Union, could ever be located. This was the work of a man who, himself, had a readable history.

As St. Louis was the center if the American fur trade, Amfurco maintained its headquarters there. In that city, on company business, McKenzie met an Englishman on the lam from the tight little isle for unspecified hanky-panky. Straight remittance-man goods, he was well-educated, a stickler for correct duds, and owned a case of gout won by his devotion to port and other hopped-up wines. He said his name was J. A. Hamilton.

Whatever he had done in Limeydom, Hamilton didn't feel that St. Louis was far enough from the arm of retribution. McKenzie needed a bookkeeper, and the toff with the expensive disease was glad of a chance to go where neither British man nor woman was likely to look for him.

Freedom from harassment was dearly bought, though. Urban by choice, Hamilton loathed the great open spaces. Addicted to clean linen and a daily tubbing, he was repelled by the bathless Johns who in general peopled the trading post. Above all, he hated Indians. They didn't overawe Hamilton; he was in command whenever McKenzie chanced to be absent, and Larpenteur told how he had had a cannon readied for savages threatening to abuse Fort Union's hospitality.

But, as a product of civilization, he simply didn't want anything to do with those who hadn't got there yet.

What the Indians thought of Hamilton is something that their illiteracy was helpless to embalm for future inspection. The views of certain white acquaintances of the period are a matter of record, however. Discussing a fellow who preferred wines to whiskey and who bathed even on wintry days, they concluded that he could not be less than a runaway earl or duke.

Yet Fort Union's unbending exile did find some consolation prizes there. McKenzie maintained a cellar which enabled Hamilton to keep his gout at par; and not infrequently the post was visited by denizens of the world perforce abandoned by the Upper Missouri's peer. As African safaris were not yet in vogue, wealthy sportsmen crossed the Atlantic to have a go at the wild beasts of the Wild West. McKenzie had the cultural address to make a pleasing host; and the passed word that de luxe hospitality was to be had near the mouth of the Yellowstone insured the coming of other *haut ton* pluggers of bison.

One of these was Prince Maximilian of Wied. At other points an interesting work, too, his *Travels in the Interior of North America* is remarkable for showing that there was one chink in Hamilton's anti-Western armor. The Britisher had become so interested in the character and career of Hugh Glass that he had written an article, based on interviews with the adventurer, which he intended for publication.

No shooting star ever did a better job of dazzling once and vanishing. Other than Maximilian's, there is no reference to the work. Nor was it seemingly ever published, although destiny gave Hugh's biographer a chance to put the item in print.

A few years after he had entertained Maximilian by a reading of his effort, Hamilton learned from somebody that the heat was partially off. If it wasn't as yet safe for him to go home, he could leave a region where port rated as a poor try at making moonshine, and lead a metropolitan life in St. Louis. Resuming his correct surname of Palmer, he hurried to the city at the other end of the Missouri, where he operated as cashier of the American Fur Company until gout finally lagged him, late in 1840.

His manuscript may have survived him; but it has not been found in either Columbia or Albion, whither some of the author's effects were known to have been sent. Unless it should somewhere be unearthed, that is all that can be told. James Archdale Hamilton Palmer, of Chipping Norton, Oxfordshire, England, had a chance to be a venerated contributor to the literature of the region he despised; but for reasons unknown, he muffed it.

It was in 1833 that Prince Maximilian audited the remittance man's work, which was topical because of a chain of recent events. The first of these was the building of a new Amfurco post called Fort Cass. Of this station Nathaniel Wyeth noted, in one of his journals dealing with trips to and from Oregon, that it "stands about 3 miles below the mouth of the Bighorn on the east (right) bank of the Yellowstone River, is about 130 ft. square, made of sapling cottonwood pickets with two bastions at extreme corners and was erected in the fall of 1832."

Also known as Tulloch's Fort, because such was the name of the builder, Fort Cass was established especially for the Crow trade. While the members of that tribe bragged, rather than confessed, that they would steal anything not riveted in place, they were in the main friendly to whites. Their country was considered a safe one, at least in the winter, when the scalp hunters of other nations normally stayed in their own bailiwicks.

Following the burning of their villages, though, the Arikaras had walked wide of standard Indian procedure. They had neither tried to rebuild the old huddles of lodges nor founded new towns in the area claimed as their own. Briefly settled near the Mandans, they had reverted from the comparatively high state of civilization they had attained. Once credited with being the canniest builders and farmers on the Plains, they had joined the wandering tepee dwellers.

With a difference, though. However overlapping with rival claims, the other tribes had domains which they thought of as their homelands. No longer possessed of patriotism on their own account, the Rees trespassed everywhere, and at all seasons. Seemingly in a constant state of fury, too, they were on no better terms with most fellow savages than they were with white men.

Some of these untiring hatchetmen were in Crow country in the winter of 1832-1833. So was Hugh Glass, who had chosen Tulloch's Fort as his cold-weather base. Ed Rose, who had likewise been with Ashley in 1823, was also there at the time.

Nobody has been able to name the day on which Glass, Rose and a chap named Menard took a one-way walk through the gate of Fort Cass, but a fair guess is that its place on the calendar was early in 1833. In the territory of a friendly tribe, and with the post right at their back, the trappers strolled down the frozen Yellowstone with the confidence of men hunting in the woodlot of a farm. But the Rees were waiting.

Flagg, who had followed Glass as far as the Missouri headwaters region, lost track of him at the last moment. He assumed that Hugh had been done away with, in the course of a trip up the Yellowstone, but only because he wasn't again located: "As to Glass, he was never again heard of and doubtless fell a victim at last, after a hundred escapes and warnings, to his own wild temerity."

Yount knew that Hugh had been ambushed, by members of the tribe which had four other times failed to have his scalp to dance around. He wasn't in position, though, to give Clark the clear picture of what happened which Maximilian obtained when he was at Fort Union not many months later: "Old Glass, with two companions, had gone from Ft. Cass to hunt beavers on the Yellow Stone, and as they were crossing the river on the ice farther down, they were all three shot, scalped and plundered by a war party of thirty Arikaras, who were concealed on the opposite bank."

The Prince furthermore knew that Glass had been soon avenged by the Johnson Gardner who was darkly remembered by officers of the Hudson's Bay Company. Although it was destroyed in a boat fire before he could display it in Germany, Maximilian wrote that he had been given what Gardner assured him was a scalp of one of the Rees who had slain Hugh.

Probably his nibs of Wied did have one of the scalps taken from the Rees because "one of them had Old Glass's knife, and his rifle had also been seen in the possession of these Indians." But what Johnson Gardner didn't tell a wealthy foreigner, from whom he no doubt expected a handsome consideration in return for his "gift" of human hair, was that it had been wrenched loose while its owner was still alive.

In different parts of his book Maximilian offers two somewhat contradictory versions of how Gardner said he did away with two of Hugh's assassins. Yet the truth was told in a letter which one John F. A. Sanford wrote to Superintendent of Indian Affairs William Clark. After passing the information that Glass, Rose and Menard had been killed and scalped by Arikaras, Sanford declared that "John Soy Gardner caught up with a couple of the murderers a few weeks later and burned them to death."

That this was generally known, in the West, was proved by what Flagg was told. If the author in question wasn't quite sure what had happened to Hugh, himself, he did know that Rees were suspected, and that something had been done about the suspicion:

"Nothing was now heard of Glass for several months. At length a party of four Erickeraw Indians came to the encampment of a company of hunters on the banks of the Powee river, and on one of these was seen several articles of clothing, which from their peculiar character were known to have belonged to Glass. The savages were immediately seized, and on declaring entire ignorance of the fate of the hunter, one of the party was released with the assurance, that unless he returned within twenty-four hours with Glass in safety, his three companions who remained as hostages should be burned at the stake. The prescribed period passed away without the messenger's appearance, and being now sure that the unfortunate hunter had been murdered by the savages then in their hands, the order was given by the leader of the party named Gardiner to burn them alive!"

Taken in advance, their scalps were saved from incineration, and so Gardner had one to bestow on Maximilian. Flagg, however, knew of a windup not mentioned by anyone else: "Not long afterwards Gardiner himself fell into the hands of the Erickeraws, who inflicted upon him the same dreadful death."

With Hugh dead, his murder requited and his avenger slain in turn, nothing remains to wonder about except the fate of the rifle which stood to him as next of kin. It had been seen in Arikara hands, but what later became of it is as little known as the whereabouts of J. A. H. Palmer's biographical work. It might still exist, unrecognized. Passing from Ree hands back to a member of a frontier generation who had no means of knowing who had once loved it, the weapon could conceivably now be a part of some collector's arsenal of obsolete firearms.

If that is the case, it will remain incognito. Or it will unless Palmer's manuscript, eventually found, reveals the name of the gunsmith and other now unknown earmarks.

The manuscript could also tell what the age of the man long referred to as "Old Glass" really was, when he was killed. As he must have pushed past fifty, and may have been closer to five dozens of years, a tribute which would have disgusted them must be given to the Rees. Although bulging with uncut venom, they were kind to Hugh, in launching the volley which brought him undawdling death.

He could not have long continued to meet the harsh demands of life as he liked to live it. He died, too, just before it became clear that the era of the free trapper was on its way to where other days have gone.

McKenzie's not long postponed success in taking over, and downscaling, the mountain fur trade was but one of the changes which soon made Hugh's preferred way of life a has-been. Missionaries became ambitious of telling Northwestern Indians about Biblical characters with dubious morals, and wagons began scarring South Pass with the ruts of the Oregon Trail. The men who now nursed pilgrims, of both sexes, on inchworm journeys along a fixed line of march, had once dashed, untethered, about their country.

They were put to sorry shifts by a European trend which first became noticeable in 1834. In that year, cloth hats had begun to supplant fur ones as the headgear of the well-dressed man. The market for beaver began slipping as of that moment, and it never regained its health.

But early in 1833, none of these blights had uglied the outlook for mountain men. When Hugh was buried in an unfound grave beside the Yellowstone, pristine wilderness and an unlimited fur market were still viewed as changeless verities.

As Glass never had to make the adjustments forced on so many of his fellows, he is the purest known example of the American in buckskin. Daniel Boone did not at all rival him. Boone was always on the fringe of pioneer settlement, while his repeatedly proved ambition was to be a great landholder. Glass functioned when and where settlement wasn't yet dreamed of, and he had no more use for a tie to any piece of real estate than he had for the leg-irons of organized society.

In that corner Imperial Rome, and in this one Hugh. There was a long drift away from the community-building spirit, brought to the New World from the Old. It found its ebb in the boom times of beaver trapping, and its epitome in a man whose story was as primal as the fear of falling.

It is not watered by any tinge of romance, patriotism, or sense of owed obligation. It is undiluted by the spirit of derring-do, the desire for wealth, an ambition for honors, or any other feeling with one eye cocked for applause or envy. It springs only from a hard-mouthed will to thrive again, in the face of cataclysm.

Older literatures have saved nothing like it. For by the time Sumerians had begun saving tales in cuneiform, the wilderness had been left so far behind that any remembered prowlers of it could be seen only through the smoky lenses of myth. The world had to wait another six thousand years before the lost chance turned up again. Then the American plunge westward made something besides savages at home in the primordial — and this time literacy was more or less watching.

Other cuttings from American history could be cited as general cases in point. But only one is absolute. There was once a civilized, modern man who was thrust as far back in dawn living conditions as Pithecanthropus, and there left desperately crippled.

The tale of what he did thereafter is splintered by differing reportings; and it must be pieced together with the aid of side remarks sifted from documents dealing with other matters. Yet the principal events can be clearly followed. However fragmentary its form, the narrative is a great one. It is likewise, according to the verdict returned with this appraisal, a thoroughly true one. It is the story of Hugh Glass, pirate, Pawnee and mountain man.

Acknowledgments

ΛΛΛΛΛΛΛ

SPECIAL THANKS are herewith tendered to Alan D. Covey and Frank A. Schneider for putting the facilities of the library of Arizona State University, Tempe, Arizona, at the disposal of a layman, and to Herbert H. Beckwith, of the same institution, for implementing library exchange service.

Thanks for courteous co-operation in supplying information and source material are also extended to the following persons and the institutions they represent:

Aubrey L. Haines, Historian, Yellowstone National Park; B. Sims, Free Library of Philadelphia, Pennsylvania; Miss Mary K. Dempsey, Historical Society of Montana, Helena, Montana; Harry Anderson, South Dakota Historical Society, Pierre, South Dakota; Merle W. Wells, Idaho Historical Society, Boise, Idaho; Archibald Hanna, Yale University Library, New Haven, Connecticut; Mrs. Barbara Elkins, Oregon Historical Society, Portland, Oregon; Mrs. J. K. Shiskin, Museum of New Mexico, Santa Fe, New Mexico; John Barr Tompkins, Bancroft Library, Berkeley, California; Miss Haydée Noya, Henry E. Huntington Library, San Marino, California; Mrs. Frances H. Stadler, Missouri Historical Society, St. Louis, Missouri; Mrs. Marguerite Cooley and Joseph Miller, Arizona State Department of Library and Archives, Phoenix, Arizona; Colton Storm, Newberry Library, Chicago, Illinois; Mrs. Yndia Moore, Arizona Pioneers Historical Society, Tucson, Arizona; Marcus A. McCorison, American Antiquarian Society, Worcester, Massachusetts; Mrs. N. L. Johnson, Louisville Free Public Library, Louisville, Kentucky; Robert W. Richmond, Kansas State Historical Society, Topeka, Kansas; Miss Margaret Rose, State Historical Society of North Dakota, Bismarck, North Dakota; Mrs. Ruth J. Bradley, Wyoming State Archives and Historical Department, Cheyenne, Wyoming; A. M. Gibson, University of Oklahoma Library, Norman, Oklahoma; John James, Jr., Utah State Historical Society, Salt Lake City, Utah; Donald F. Danker, Nebraska State Historical Society, Lincoln, Nebraska; James J. Heslin, New York Historical Society, New York City; and anonymous but equally helpful operatives at the St. Louis Public Library and the Library of the University of Chicago.

Bibliography

Abel, Annie Heloise. *Tarbeau's Narrative of Loisel's Expedition to the Upper Missouri.* Norman, Oklahoma, 1959.

Alter, J. Cecil. *James Bridger: Trapper, Frontiersman, Scout and Guide.* Columbus, Ohio, 1951.

Anonymous, "Old Glass," in *St. Louis Evening Gazette,* March 17, 1840. St. Louis, Missouri.

Berry, Don. *A Majority of Scoundrels: An Informal History of the Rocky Mountain Fur Company.* New York, New York, 1961.

Blair, Walter, and Meine, Franklin J. *Half Horse and Half Alligator: The Growth of the Mike Fink Legend.* Chicago, Illinois, 1956.

Bonner, T. D. *Life and Adventures of James P. Beckwourth.* New York, 1856.

Botkin, B. A. *A Treasury of Western Folk Lore.* New York, 1951.

Brackenridge, H. M. *Journal of a Voyage Up the Missouri.* Cleveland, Ohio, 1904.

Bradbury, John. *Travels in the Interior of America.* Cleveland, 1904.

Brown, Mark. *The Plainsmen of the Yellowstone.* New York, 1961.

Burt, Struthers. *Powder River.* New York, 1938.

Caesar, Gene. *King of the Mountain Men: The Life of Jim Bridger.* New York, 1961.

Camp, Charles L. (Ed.) *The Chronicles of George C. Yount.*

California Historical Quarterly, 1923, Vol. II. Berkeley, California.

———. *The D. T. P. Letters: Essays for Henry R. Wagner,* San Francisco, California, 1947.

———. *James Clyman, Frontiersman.* Portland, Oregon, 1960.

Campbell, Walter S. *Mountain Men.* Boston, Massachusetts, 1937.

———. *Jim Bridger, Mountain Man.* New York, 1946.

Cattermole, E. G. *Famous Frontiersmen, Pioneers and Scouts.* Chicago, 1883.

Celand, Robert Glass. *This Reckless Breed of Men.* New York, 1950.

Chittenden, Hiram M. *The American Fur Trade of the Far West.* 2 vols. Palo Alto, California, 1954.

Cooke, Philip St. George. "Some Incidents in the Life of Hugh Glass, a Hunter of the Missouri River," in *St. Louis Beacon,* December 2 and December 9, 1830. St. Louis.

———. *Scenes and Adventures in the Army.* Philadelphia, Pennsylvania, 1857.

Dale, H. C. *The Ashley-Smith Explorations.* Cleveland, 1918.

DeVoto, Bernard. *Across the Wide Missouri.* Boston, 1947.

———. *The Course of Empire.* Boston, 1952.

Dictionary of American Biography. 20 vols. New York, 1928-1936.

Duffus, Robert L. *The Santa Fe Trail.* New York, 1930.

Eller, W. H. *The Arickara Conquest of 1823.* Nebraska State Historicial Society: Transactions and Reports. Vol. 5. Lincoln, Nebraska, 1893.

Ellison, William H. (Ed.) *The Life and Adventures of George Nidever.* Berkeley, 1937.

Favour, Alpheus E. *Old Bill Williams, Mountain Man.* Chapel Hill, North Carolina, 1936.

Ferris, W. A. *Life in the Rocky Mountains.* Denver, Colorado, 1940.

Flagg, Edmund. "Adventures at the Headwaters of the Missouri," in Louisville *Literary News-Letter,* September 7, 1839. Louisville, Kentucky.

Frost, Donald McKay. *Notes on General Ashley, the Overland Trail and South Pass.* American Antiquarian Society, Proceedings, Vol. 54. Worcester, Massachusetts, 1945.

Ghent, W. J. *The Early Far West: A Narrative Outline.* New York, 1936.

Grant, Blanche. *When Old Trails Were New: The Story of Taos.* New York, 1934.

Gregg, Josiah. *Commerce of the Prairies;* 2 vols. New York, 1844.

Haines, Aubrey L. (Ed.) *Osborne Russell's Journal of a Trapper.* Portland, Oregon, 1955.

Hall, James. "The Missouri Trapper." "Letters from the West," No. XIV, in the *Port Folio,* March, 1825. Philadelphia, Pennsylvania.

Hodge, Frederick W. *Handbook of American Indians.* 2 vols. Washington, L. C., 1907-1910.

Holmes, Reuben. *The Five Scalps. Glimpses of the Past,* Vol. V. St. Louis, 1938.

Inman, Henry. *The Old Santa Fe Trail.* New York, 1899.

Irving, John Treat. *Indian Sketches Taken During an Expedition to the Pawnee Tribes,* 1833. Norman, Oklahoma, 1955.

Irving, Washington. *Astoria, or Anecdotes of an Enterprise Beyond the Rockies.* Philadelphia, 1836.

————. *A Tour of the Prairies.* Norman, Oklahoma, 1956.

James, Edwin. *Account of an Expedition from Pittsburgh to the Rocky Mountains . . . under the Command of Major Stephen H. Long.* Philadelphia, 1823.

Larpenteur, Charles. *Forty Years a Fur Trader on the Upper Missouri.* Chicago, 1933.

Lavender, David. *Bent's Fort.* Garden City, New York, 1954.

LeRoy, Bruce. *H. M. Chittenden, a Western Epic.* Tacoma, Washington, 1961.

Lewis, Meriwether. *History Of the Expedition Under the Command of Captains Lewis and Clark To the Sources Of the Missouri; Thence Across the Rockies And Down*

Bibliography

Bibliography

Bibliography

the *River Columbia To the Pacific Ocean*. Philadelphia, 1814.

Luttig, John C. *Journal of a Fur Trading Expedition to the Upper Missouri*. Edited by Stella M. Drumm. St. Louis, 1920.

McElroy, Robert McNutt. *The Winning of the Far West*. New York, 1914.

Morgan, Dale L. *Jedediah Smith and the Opening of the West*. Indianapolis, 1953.

Mumey, Nolie. *The Life of Jim Baker*. Glendale, California, 1931.

Myers, John Myers. *The Alamo*. New York, 1948.

———. *The Deaths of the Bravos*. Boston, 1962.

Neihardt, John G. *The Song of Hugh Glass*. New York, 1915.

———. *The Splendid Wayfaring*. New York, 1920.

North Dakota Historical Quarterly. Vols. 3 and 4. Bismarck, North Dakota, 1928-1930.

Nute, Grace Lee. *Calendar of the American Fur Company's Papers*. Washington, D. C., 1945.

Ogden, Peter Skene [putative author]. *Traits of American Indian Life and Character*. London, 1853.

Pattie, James Ohio. *The Personal Narrative of James O. Pattie of Kentucky . . . Through the Vast Regions between That Place and the Pacific Ocean*. Edited by Timothy Flint. Cincinnati, Ohio, 1831.

Pike, Zebulon Montgomery. *An Account of Expeditions to the Sources of the Mississippi . . . the Arkansas, the Kans, La Platte and Pierre Jaune Rivers . . . and a Tour Through the Interior Parts of New Spain*. Philadelphia, 1810.

Potts, Daniel T. *Early Yellowstone and Western Experiences: Yellowstone Nature Notes*, Vol. XXI (September-October, 1947).

Randall, Randolph C. *Authors of the Port Folio Revealed by the Hall Files. American Literature*, Vol. 11. Durham, North Carolina, 1940.

Ruxton, George F. *Adventures in New Mexico and the Rocky Mountains.* London, 1847.
————. *Life in the Far West.* New York, 1849.

Sage, Rufus. *Scenes in the Rocky Mountains.* Philadelphia, 1847.

Saxon, Lyle. *Lafitte the Pirate.* New York, 1930.

Smurr, J. W. (Ed.) *Historical Essays on Montana and the Northwest.* Helena, Montana, 1957.

South Dakota Historical Collections. Vols. I and II. Pierre, South Dakota, 1902-1903.

Stone, Irving. *Men to Match My Mountains.* Garden City, New York, 1956.

Sullivan, Maurice. *The Travels of Jedediah Smith.* Santa Ana, California, 1934.

Sunder, John E. *Bill Sublette, Mountain Man.* Norman, Oklahoma, 1959.

Thwaites, Reuben Gold (Ed.). *Travels in the Interior of North America by Maximilian, Prince of Wied.* Cleveland, 1906.

Triplett, Frank. *Conquering the Wilderness.* New York, 1883.

Vestal, Stanley (See Campbell, Walter S.)

Victor, Frances F. *The River of the West.* Hartford, Connecticut, 1870.

Warren, Harris Gaylord. *The Sword Was Their Passport.* Baton Rouge, Louisiana, 1943.

Webb, Walter Prescott. *The Great Plains.* New York, 1931.

Wellman, Paul E. *Death on Horseback.* Philadelphia, 1947.

Williams, Chauncey P. *Lone Elk: The Life Story of Old Bill Williams.* Denver, Colorado, 1935.

Wissler, Clark. *The American Indian.* New York, 1931.

Young, Otis E. (Ed.) *The First Military Escort on the Santa Fe Trail . . . From the Journal and Reports of Major Bennet Riley and Lieutenant Philip St. George Cooke. Glendale, California, 1952.*